HANGING THE
PEACHTREE
BANDIT

THE TRUE TALE OF ATLANTA'S
INFAMOUS FRANK DUPRE

TOM HUGHES

Charleston — London

THE
History
PRESS

Published by The History Press
Charleston, SC 29403
www.historypress.net

Copyright © 2014 by Tom Hughes
All rights reserved

First published 2014

Manufactured in the United States

ISBN 978.1.62619.416.8

Library of Congress CIP data applied for.

Contents

Introduction

Betty told DuPre, "I want a diamond ring."
DuPre told Betty, "Baby, I'll get you most anything."

Days before Christmas 1921, Frank DuPre, a jobless eighteen-year-old, fortified with moonshine and carrying a pocket pistol, entered a jewelry store on Atlanta's famous Peachtree Street. Minutes later, he dashed away clutching a diamond ring. Behind him he left a dead Pinkerton detective. Frank kept his promise to his sweetheart of six days, Betty Andrews. The legend of the "Peachtree Bandit" was born.

For weeks, embattled police "sleuths" searched in vain for the "desperado." Frank was arrested in Detroit, days after posting a letter to the *Atlanta Constitution* mocking the local detectives as a bunch of "boneheads." In shackles, cowering and chain-smoking, Frank was returned to a city "in the grip of crime." Thousands were at the Union Depot when his train arrived. John Boykin, the zealous local prosecutor, declared, "Of course, I shall be seeking the death penalty." In a fortnight, DuPre was tried, convicted and sentenced to hang.

An increasingly bitter but remarkably advanced struggle ensued to save Frank's life. Was he a cold-blooded killer or a "high-grade moron?" Though the Peachtree Bandit eventually hanged on September 1, 1922, his case led to the establishment of Georgia's first-ever Anti-Noose League and major changes in the state's capital punishment laws.

This is the factual recounting of an American tragedy. Additionally, the squalid tale of Frank and Betty engendered a blues tradition. Though two white teenagers, their story has become a predominantly African American blues classic. First recorded by Blind Willie Walker in 1930, the traditional "DuPree Blues" has been recorded by artists as disparate as Harry Belafonte and the Grateful Dead.

This is as much a story of Atlanta as the fictional tale of Scarlett and Rhett. This is the true and tragic story of Betty and DuPre.

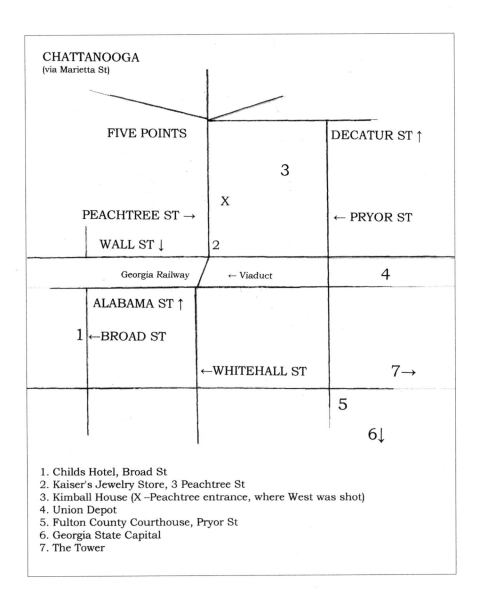

CHATTANOOGA
(via Marietta St)

FIVE POINTS

DECATUR ST ↑

3

X

PEACHTREE ST →

← PRYOR ST

WALL ST ↓

2

Georgia Railway   ← Viaduct   4

ALABAMA ST ↑

1 ←BROAD ST

←WHITEHALL ST   7→

5

6↓

1. Childs Hotel, Broad St
2. Kaiser's Jewelry Store, 3 Peachtree St
3. Kimball House (X –Peachtree entrance, where West was shot)
4. Union Depot
5. Fulton County Courthouse, Pryor St
6. Georgia State Capital
7. The Tower

A map of downtown Atlanta, 1921–22. *Drawn by the author.*

Chapter 1

"A Scene of Terror and Excitement"

Where the southern end of Peachtree met the northern end of Whitehall was the heart of Atlanta's shopping district. At the start of the twentieth century, the streets were still separated by a dangerous grade-level railroad crossing. While the railroads had truly established Atlanta, they also created an infamous "sewer of smoke" cleaving the city. In 1901, the first viaduct was built to span the tracks. While the smoke, whistles and general cacophony continued one level below, Peachtree and Whitehall were linked at last in "a scene of magnificent structures, an attractive business locality and a thoroughfare of convenience and safety, connecting together the north and south sides of Atlanta."[1] Streetcar bells clanged, motorcars puttered and pedestrians scurried amidst them all.

In 1921, the two streets offered something for every budget, from five-and-dime stores to the high-end emporia of the rival mercantile giants, the Messrs High and Rich. The newest attraction was the Peachtree Arcade, Atlanta's first shopping mall. Just north of the viaduct, the three-level arcade stretched between Peachtree and Broad and featured dress shops, perfumeries and even a gunsmith. And Santa, too. Mr. Claus arrived on December 10, 1921. Also, the city's first-ever public Christmas tree was erected in the arcade. It was hailed as the "best advertizing stunt ever pulled off in Atlanta." Holiday shopping was in full swing.

Directly across from the arcade, at 3 Peachtree Street on the ground floor of the Peters Building, was Nat Kaiser's Jewelry. Its motto was: "Ask anybody, Nat Kaiser will save you money on Diamonds." Kaiser's sidewalk clock read a few minutes past one o'clock on the crisp sunny afternoon of Thursday, December 15. Inside, the store was busy. A young man entered, brushing past other shoppers, and approached salesclerk Evelyn Phillips. She stood behind a large L-shaped glass display counter. The fellow said he was about to get married and was in search of a diamond ring. Mrs. Phillips pleasantly assured the young man, "We have several here." The young shopper appeared well dressed in a grey suit and a tie beneath a grey plaid topcoat. However, he wore a more plebian cloth "newsboy" cap. His eyes also bore a curious squint. Mrs. Phillips thought she would show him some more affordable rings. But after a quick dismissive glance, the fellow pronounced, "They won't do at all. I want to see that big ring in your window." In a friendly way, the saleswoman whispered that that particular ring was quite expensive. "Did I ask you the price?" came the abrupt reply. Mrs. Phillips said it would be just a moment. "Mr. Ullman will be out to help you."

Nat Ullman came out from his manager's office, pausing to speak with another young man on the sales floor. This second man took a position blocking the doorway to Peachtree. Ullman greeted the young customer and repeated that the ring in the window was very costly indeed. Again, the shopper was adamant: "It's your business to show it to me if I want to buy it—and I do." Ullman returned with the ring, placing it on a velvet cloth. It was a 3.25-carat diamond in a green-gold setting, priced at $2,500 (a $30,000 ring in 2014).[2] The fellow eyed it carefully and then excitedly said, "I'll take it." Grabbing the ring in his left hand, he turned for the door, which was blocked by the Kaiser's detective. The two men were equal in size, and the detective at first had the upper hand, pushing the thief back into the store, knocking over and shattering a glass partition. Then there were gunshots. From the right pocket of his overcoat, the thief had drawn a pistol, pressed it to the side of his opponent and fired upward. The detective gasped and staggered farther into the store, pleading for a doctor, and collapsed.

The gunman, pistol in his right hand, ring in his left, bolted into Peachtree, turning right and running north. From behind him, a pursuing cry was heard from Kaiser's: "Stop him!" Pushing his way through a sidewalk filled with shoppers, the shooter reached the motor entrance to the Kimball House. Beneath a canopy, a door opened into a long and brightly lit hallway leading some one hundred feet to a revolving door, beyond which was the hotel lobby.

As the shooter entered this hallway, two men emerged from the revolving door opposite, walking toward Peachtree. The young man stumbled past them, losing his balance and falling to the floor. Behind him, the crowd of shouting pursuers appeared. One of the businessmen turned toward the fallen man. He was shot in the head.

The chasers now fell back in fear. The young man, on his feet again, spun through the revolving door into the hotel's celebrated lobby, an atrium brightened by a hammered-glass ceiling seven stories above. Everything was decorated for the holiday. The young man hollered out that a man had been shot out in the corridor. The sound of the gunshot had clearly been heard—the hatcheck girl was on the floor, and the ladies at the Christmas Seals table were now under that table. The shooter did not linger but took the doorway to the left into the hotel's billiard room.

It was undeniably the nicest pool hall in town. Yet the afternoon tables were hardly busy, with merely a few rack boys and desultory loungers hanging about. Into their midst burst this panting young fellow obviously on the run. Well, he couldn't hide out there. A regular snapped, "Beat it." The lad took his exit. Recrossing the lobby, past an immense roaring fireplace, he entered one of the small shops that opened out on to Wall Street. Witnesses later told police that the man in a grey overcoat came out of the Kimball's

"A View of Peachtree Street Looking North from the Viaduct." See the Kaiser's sidewalk clock (right) and the Kimball House entryway ahead. Imperial Postcard Co. *Author's collection.*

haberdashery and crossed the railroad tracks at the Union Depot, where all trace of him was lost.

The scene in the heart of Atlanta's downtown can be easily imagined. Police whistles split the air. Ambulances, sirens wailing, maneuvered through choked streets. Panicked shoppers milled about. Confusion prevailed. At Kaiser's, Irby Walker, a Pinkerton store detective, had died in the arms of a Kaiser's salesman. Dr. Spencer Folsom arrived aboard the Grady Hospital ambulance to pronounce him dead. Walker was only twenty-eight. Married, he lived with his wife and seven-year-old daughter in Candler Park. It had been his first day on the "special holiday detail" at Kaiser's.

At the Kimball House, a great crowd gathered in the narrow corridor around the downed man. "Why, it's Comptroller West," someone asserted. Graham West, the comptroller of the city of Atlanta, had been returning to City Hall. The bullet struck West in the jaw but missed major arteries, and while it was quite a ghastly wound, he would recover.

Downtown remained a scene of "terror and excitement." There had been at least seven police officers on duty in that block of Peachtree alone, and yet the gunman had eluded them all. The police arrested Berry Cline, the poolroom lounger who had told the bandit to beat it. Cline insisted he had never seen the fellow before but chased him off because he thought he was a "troublemaker." Cline was released.

Mayor James Key arrived, promising his full attention to the tragic affair. Police Chief James Beavers had taken command and was joined by Frank Fenn, the director of the Atlanta Pinkerton Agency in the Hurt Building, who described Walker as one of his best young operatives.

Police were quickly posted at all the rail stations. With roughly 124 passenger and 378 freight trains moving through Atlanta each day, it was the most likely route of escape.

By late afternoon, a "lookout telegram" was issued with a detailed description of the suspect. Mrs. Phillips, described in the *Georgian* as a "pretty woman clerk," was too shaken to assist the police. However, her colleague, Donald Drukenmiller, who claimed to have made "a special study of criminals and criminal types," had gotten a good look at the man. Drukenmiller told the cops that the thief was "undoubtedly a professional." He was about twenty-five years old, stood five foot six and weighed 135 pounds. He wore an overcoat of a thick weave, with a pepper-and-salt effect; it was single breasted to the knees. He wore a grey cap. The bandit, Drukenmiller concluded, had a "typical crook's face. His features were sharp, particularly the nose. His eyes were dark and piercing with the pupils slightly out of alignment. His eyebrows were black and heavy. His hair was dark and cut medium length. He was of fair complexion with a slightly olive tinge. It was the complexion of a man that does not stay outdoors much but not the complexion of a drug addict. He talks quietly with a slight twang." Drukenmiller had good reason to know the face—he had chased the gunman, and he believed the bullet that struck Comptroller West had actually been meant for him.

Police were advised that the bandit was armed and dangerous: "See him and shoot." The Jeweler's Security Alliance, created in tandem with the Pinkerton agency, wired a similar description to its members: "The suspect is between 22 and 25, roughly five feet six, 140 pounds. The murderer was apparently well-educated and made a neat appearance, but has the countenance of a dangerous looking character. He was wearing a gray and brown plaid overcoat and a gray cap with a long visor."

The overcoat became the first headline-catching detail in the manhunt. The city awoke Friday to read that the police were baffled in their pursuit for the "Grey Overcoat Bandit." Trying to find a killer among all the men wearing a grey overcoat in mid-December, even in temperate Atlanta, would not be easy. So many men were stopped for questioning that the *Constitution* suggested that gentlemen owning such a coat were "safest at [their] own firesides." Similarly, other men were suspected simply because their eyes were "out of alignment." Detectives made the rounds of the poolrooms, barbershops and "soft drink parlors," surveying the coats, eyes and hair styles of the denizens of such loafer hangouts but without result. The Civitans posted the first reward of $1,000; Comptroller West was a leading member of the club. West was recovering. The bullet had "bored a hole thru the lower part of his chin bone" and emerged to cause a slight flesh wound to a shoulder. The "unusually courageous" patient was conscious and would make a full recovery. Meanwhile, Irby Walker's body had been taken to Rutledge, Alabama, for burial.

The manhunt produced another misstep. Police announced that they were looking for a race car driver named "Dirt Track" Kelly. It turned out that Kelly had been in Birmingham, Alabama, on Thursday, and, in his words, he "humped it" to Atlanta to establish his innocence. Drukenmiller was brought in and assured police Kelly was not the bandit. This was just more ammunition for the expected outcry from the press denouncing the police for their incompetence and inability to protect the public. The head of the city's police commission described the performance of Beavers's department as "pathetic." The *Macon Telegraph* reported, "Atlanta's enormously increased wave of crime has created quite a tense excitement all over the city." The correspondent for the *Savannah Press* informed coastal readers that the shooting had loosed "a storm of protest over police incompetence and inefficiency." There were new calls for the removal of Chief Beavers. In fact, the Savannah daily reported, "It seemed likely today that the whole city government may go on the rocks unless the police department is reorganized from top to bottom."

Late Friday, the harried police got their first lead. Heavily armed lawmen headed for Chattanooga but arrived in Tennessee too late. The bandit had already left there by train for Norfolk. And there, too, he slipped through a trap. "The escape of the bandit from the police in a number of cities has been one of the most sensational in recent criminal annals. From time to time, reports that he was all but captured have been followed by information that he cleverly eluded the outstretched hand of the law and is still at large." At least the sleuths now had the desperado's name. Frank DuPre was now "being hunted by every method and by every means known to detective science."

Chapter 2

"In the Grip of Crime"

On the morning of Thursday, December 15, 1921, just hours before the shooting at Kaiser's, the *Constitution* headlined, "HOLDUP & THEFT EPIDEMIC HOLDING ATLANTA IN GRIP." There had been a dozen holdups the previous day. "Never before," the paper howled, "has there been such a wave of highway robberies." The community was demanding action, but "the police are absolutely unable to cope."

Hours later, the city's two afternoon papers hit the streets with news of the most shocking crime yet—the midday stickup of a Peachtree jewelry store. The *Georgian* declared, "TWO MEN SHOT DOWN IN PEACHTREE STREET HOLDUP." To be shot down outside some Decatur Street dive was one thing; when it happened on Peachtree, it sent a frisson of fear through the city.

Crime in Atlanta was not new—vice, moonshining and gambling were chronic problems. Atlanta was known nationally as a "mecca for a slippery gang of crooks."[3] In 1921, Fulton County solicitor general John Boykin took on the city's infamous "Swindle Syndicate," a bunco gang that ran a real-life version of the Newman-Redford operation from *The Sting*. The racketeers, based at the San Souci hotel on Cone Street, conned their victims with rigged card games, phony horse race result tickers and "can't miss" bogus stock trading.

Much more frightening was random violent crime. In 1920, in a city of 200,000 people, Atlanta police, with a force of 300 (including the first policewomen) made 20,000 arrests. In 1917, there were 750 felonies in Atlanta. In the first half of 1921, there were more than 1,000. Only Memphis had more murders per capita.[4] The *Constitution* wondered whether Georgia was in the midst of a "killing orgy." More than three-fourths of the

First word of the "daring crime." Atlanta Georgian, *December 15, 1921.*

murders involved guns, especially the pocket pistol. "Just why any peaceful, well-meaning citizen should persist in going about his everyday affairs with a murderous pistol hidden in his hip pocket is hard to understand. But, judging from the daily news reports, many of them do."

The Peachtree shooting bolstered the belief that crime was out of control. As the 1920s began, the American press was obsessed with crime. The respected *Literary Digest* pondered "America's High Tide of Crime." The *New Republic* declared it "The Permanent Crime Wave." The theories for the crime surge were numerous and hotly debated. Some blamed postwar immigration from Europe, primarily Italian and Irish gangs bringing their feuds and secret societies to America. But the leading suspects were domestic: unemployment, Prohibition and the general social breakdown that followed the First World War. The latter was summed up as "the flapper culture."

After the war ended in 1918, the U.S. economy went into a prolonged slump. It was "the depression you've never heard of."[5] In the South, the pestiferous boll weevil made it worse. In five years, the bug took a 40 percent bite out of Georgia's cotton industry.[6] Jobs disappeared, driving more young people into the cities. In 1920, the federal government began reporting on jobs, and Atlanta was high among those cities with "serious unemployment." Mayor Key (whose Ponce De

Leon home had been burglarized) pressed the city council to accelerate contracts for street repairs to create needed employment. The (White) Christian Council launched a drive to "give a man a job today." The mayor threatened that any employers who failed to participate would be subjected to "public scorn."

There were too many idle young men hanging around Atlanta, and trouble was easy to find. These youth were variously denounced as "sidewalk sheiks, pool room loafers, hotel lobby loungers, parlor parasites and plain bums." In the Gate City, there was "trouble with a capital 'T' and that rhymes with 'P' and that stands for pool." As *The Music Man's* Harold Hill had insisted, "That game with the fifteen numbered balls is the devil's tool."[7] The 1922 Atlanta city directory listed fifty pool halls. The police periodically raided the murkier establishments under an "Idling and Loitering" ordinance. The *Constitution* applauded the police, something it did very rarely: "The authorities are to be commended for having again undertaken to rid the city of loungers and loafers. They have begun at the right place, too, in tackling the poolrooms first."

Atlanta had a well-established reputation for vice and prostitution. Police efforts to control it were ineffectual, and police corruption was believed to be a factor. Some of the city's cheaper hotels were little more than poorly disguised brothels.

Then there was Prohibition. "America's Great Experiment" is often cited as a leading contributor to the so-called carnival of crime. Ironically, proponents had argued that ending the drink trade would mean a reduction in violence. The opposite had occurred. Georgia had actually been a dry state since 1908, banning even communion wine. But Atlanta's home-rule exception allowed "near beer," and saloons proliferated. They were denounced as havens for crime and race mixing. But even these were shut down by the Eighteenth Amendment. On January 17, 1920, the near beer went down the sewers. Proponents declared that a sober America would be a safer, more peaceful America. Alas, given the opportunity to make huge profits from supplying a contraband product, there were those who rushed in to fill that void.

As 1920s historian Frederick Lewis Allen sagely observed, "Obviously there were large sections of the country in which prohibition was not prohibiting."[8] Spirituous drink was readily available in Atlanta. The city never saw the level of organized violence that occurred in the great northern cities. There were no Al Capones in Dixie. Yet the cat-and-mouse wars between the moonshiners and the lurking revenue agents were quite frequently violent. The high-speed dirt-road chase scenes are still celebrated in NASCAR lore. Enough booze got through to slake the thirst of Atlanta's toping classes. The shine was clandestinely drunk at private parties, political clubhouses or at any of the dozens of "soft drink emporia" that were supposedly restricted to selling Coca-Cola, NuGrape and lemonade. Harry Saphire, the chief federal Prohibition agent, railed against "the Atlanta whiskey interests who control whole fleets of high powered automobiles."[9] City officials had to be looking the other way. The press was also silent. Jack's Place, a "muchly-raided drinking parlor," was just doors from the *Constitution*'s newsroom.

Finally, the end of the Great War brought rapid social change. Young people were flocking to see Hollywood thrillers. Chief Beavers thought "lurid motion pictures" were ruining Atlanta's youth, who were also driving fast cars, listening to jazz music or, worse, dancing to it. There was a newly liberated young woman in America whose brazenness was summed up in the word "flapper"—even on Peachtree. The *Constitution*'s Ernie Rogers (perhaps regrettably) wrote:

> *On Peachtree Street the flappers go*
> *By the tea hounds row on row*
> *They make a multicolored show*
> *And look so sweet.*
>
> *Aromas waft from weird perfume*
> *And garments flash from fashion's loom,*
> *That's where the Georgia peaches bloom,*
> *On Peachtree Street.*
>
> *On Peachtree Street trim ankles prance*
> *Which leave a longing for the dance*
> *And in their pathway give, perchance,*
> *The eyes a treat.*
>
> *There's meaning in the shadowed glance,*
> *That strikes its mark by lucky chance,*
> *Where flames the New South's old romance*
> *On Peachtree Street.*[10]

So, as Christmas 1921 approached, Atlanta faced too much crime, too many loafers, hanging out in too many damnable pool halls, drinking easily available moonshine, toting pocket pistols and carrying on with flapper girls. On December 15, 1921, an unemployed teenager who made his nefarious plan in a poolroom and drank whiskey for courage set off with his pocket pistol to rob and kill for his flapper girl. If law enforcement needed someone to serve as an example, that someone was Frank DuPre.

Chapter 3

Frank DuPre

Abbeville, in upstate South Carolina, claims to be both cradle and deathbed of the Confederacy. In 1860, after a meeting on nearby "Secession Hill," South Carolina became the first state to leave the Union. Then, in April 1865, Jefferson Davis, in full flight, held his last cabinet meeting in Abbeville. By 1900, Abbeville was a prosperous market town with five thousand residents. The leading employer was the Abbeville Cotton Mill. An opera house and posh hotels lined the Court Square, dominated by a well-tended obelisk to the Civil War dead. The railroad was, of course, vital. Abbeville had a prized stop on the Seaboard Air Line. Atlanta was 150 miles down the tracks.

Frank DuPre was born in Abbeville in August 1903. DuPre is a Huguenot name meaning "from the meadow." Abbeville had been settled in the 1750s by Huguenots, Protestants driven out of Catholic France. The DuPres were a well-established family in Abbeville. In 1909, the local *Press & Banner* reported the marriage of William DuPre and Eleanor Eigenman, the bride breathlessly described as "the daughter of a former attendant to the Grand Duke of Karlsruhe." But Frank was unrelated to that exalted DuPre line. He was the son and grandson of blacksmiths. Frank A. DuPre, the bandit's father, was born in Charleston but had moved upstate. In 1899, in Abbeville, he married a blacksmith's daughter, Nannie Pearl Schroeder. The Schroeders were from Germany. John Schroeder worked for Seaboard Rail. Frank and Nannie Pearl DuPre had two children: Joe, the eldest, born in 1900, and Frank, born three years later.

Frank (background) with his older brother, Joe.
Courtesy of Mary Ellen DuPre-Burns, Joe's granddaughter.

The DuPre family moved to Atlanta, with the elder Frank employed as a railroad blacksmith. It was hard work—for four dollars a day, he worked the forge, tending "cherry red" fires amid the incessant din of banging steel hammers. The DuPres appear in the 1910 census: Joe was ten, and Frank was seven. They lived the longest at 412 Simpson Street, where the neighbors remembered Frank as a "sissy." He went to the local school on Davis Street. The Atlanta public schools, even those for whites only, were struggling. In 1915, the *Constitution* denounced "the deplorable conditions" at Davis Street School. Whether this was a factor or not, Frank's schooling ended in the eighth grade.

In 1916, the DuPres moved to Charleston. Frank's father found work in the shops at the new navy yard. Then, Frank's mother made her first bid to kill herself by taking laudanum. She failed but tried again a year later by drinking disinfectant. Again, the miserable woman survived. Mercifully, perhaps, Nannie Pearl was among those who died during the influenza outbreak of November 1918. She was thirty-eight, and she is buried in the DuPre plot at the Abbeville Cemetery.

After losing his wife, Frank DuPre lost his job in the naval cuts that followed the war's end. Young Frank was uprooted and traveled with his father seeking work. The available jobs were short-lived and/or underpaid. The DuPres, father and son, were back in Atlanta in 1920 living at a boardinghouse. The elder DuPre found railway work at the vast Howell Shops northwest of downtown. At seventeen, Frank found his first job at the Scenic Film Company. Atlanta entrepreneur Carl Rowntree has been called the "originator of the animated ad film." His Spring Street studio produced "animated advertizing, news picture weeklies and other commercial cinematography." Frank did odd jobs and made twenty dollars a week until he was laid off. Rowntree described Frank as a good worker, quiet and well liked. But "owing to business issues," he was let go.[11]

On December 13, 1920, Frank enlisted in the navy for four years. At the recruiting office on Forsyth Street, the medical examination was perfunctory. He was sixty-eight inches tall with "slightly below normal vision" in his left eye. He was assigned to the Hampton Roads naval base in Virginia. Frank had apparently enlisted without his father's permission. He soon requested a discharge, claiming his family had disapproved; he was needed at home to help "support his parents [sic]."[12] Meanwhile, the newly elected president, Warren Harding, who ran on a pledge of postwar austerity, cut navy manpower by 50 percent. Thus, in March 1921, Frank was discharged. It was not the last time President Harding would enter the life of Frank DuPre.

Out of uniform and out of a job, Frank returned to his father, who was then working in Charleston. But father and son were back in Atlanta by the summer of 1921. Frank was again taken on by Scenic Films, this time for only ten dollars a week—and not for long, either, as he was laid off again in July. Mr. DuPre also lost his job and decided to look for work in Birmingham. At his father's urging, Frank went back to Abbeville but found no work there either, grousing, "You have to wait for somebody to die to get a job [in Abbeville]."

Frank was back in Atlanta for October's annual Great Southeastern Fair. What young man would want to miss the fair? The extravaganza was "the great annual ten-day industrial, recreational and development event of the South." Attendance topped 200,000. There were livestock and agricultural competitions and trade shows. But mostly there were fun things to see and do. The 1921 fair featured a motorcar speed carnival, with "the nation's best dirt track pilots" racing around the lake. The midway was packed, especially by young men ogling C.A. Wortham's Beach Models, an assemblage of "pretty girls and diving nymphs." The fair also had its shadier side as the city's aforementioned "swindle syndicate" gleefully fleeced their country cousins.

Whatever money Frank had to spend at the fair was soon gone, and by late October, he was hungry and broke. On the evening of Sunday, October 30, he was at Pitts' Corner, a legendary cigar shop at Five Points. "Meet me at Pitts," the locals said. Who should pass but J.C. Reville, the husband of a first cousin. A traveling salesman, Reville was flush with cash. He was staying at Peachtree's Aragon Hotel, and he offered Frank a meal and a bed for the night. The Aragon was once the city's finest hotel, but by 1921, "its solid bulk had begun to exude an air of shabby gentility."[13] Frank spent the night and rewarded his kinsman's kindness by quietly getting out of bed and stealing Reville's watch and $140 in cash.

Curiously, Reville never reported the theft to the police or Frank's family. Had they brought some women to the room at the Aragon and Reville feared that Frank would tell his wife? This is purely speculation. Regardless, Frank's father insisted—albeit after the fact—that had Reville only gotten word to him, he would have come straight to Atlanta and dealt with it. But instead Frank had money to spend. He moved to a nicer boarding hotel, bought new clothes, saw some motion pictures and paid women for sex. But at the rate Frank was paying it out, even $140 wouldn't last forever.

Frank made no new effort to find a job. He was now another loafer moving between barbershops, lobbies and poolrooms. The associations at such "hotbeds of lawlessness" were not likely to be good ones. "These rendezvous at their worst, indeed, are the meeting places of the under-world mashers, cadets, procurers, gangsters, gunmen, thieves, and criminals of all sorts."[14] Such places were notorious seedbeds for crackbrained criminal schemes, most of which never amounted to more than overheated talk. But when the end of the Reville funds appeared near, Frank had to do something. The entry-level crime was generally purse snatching. But the risk was hardly worth the reward. You might well be chased down and knocked about by bystanders and find yourself on some brutal chain gang. In the pool halls, he heard of other options for a fellow willing to "pull a job."

Davis & Freeman Jewelers was on Whitehall, across from Rich's. It sponsored an annual silver cup competed for by Atlanta's top country club golfers; young Bobby Jones won it in 1920. On December 3, 1921, Frank went into the store and boldly grabbed two rings and a platinum cup. "In an instant, he was gone," a clerk told police. So bad was crime downtown that this daring daylight heist received only the briefest mention in the papers. A more shocking crime the same day had overshadowed everything. Charlie Crawford, a black laundryman, was passing by Goldberg's grocery on Woodward Street and heard a call for help. He found the shopkeeper struggling with a thief. This second man turned his pistol on Crawford and shot him dead. The killer escaped. "Touching tributes" were offered for the colored man who died for a white man. The Atlanta National Bank opened one of the most "unusual accounts" in its history—the Charlie Crawford Fund. (Contributions: $55.65.)

The police would later claim that DuPre was the man who murdered Crawford. But the grocer, who survived, failed to identify Frank as the shooter. On December 3, the day Crawford died, Frank had not yet purchased his gun. He bought the pistol two days later with his takings from the Davis & Freeman job. He had hocked the rings with the assistance of Jack Worth, a sometimes bill collector, pants presser and occasional fence. A bootlegger had told Frank that Worth was the man to see. They met in a pool hall, where Frank showed Worth the two stolen rings (the platinum cup is lost to history). The larger stone was worth about $1,200 and the smaller one $700. For the smaller ring, Worth offered Frank $125. Frank wanted $150, but Worth would go no higher. Frank agreed, but he would want at least $500 for the larger stone. Worth explained that he was only a small-time operator but that he "knew a guy." Frank went with Worth to the Georgia Savings & Trust Company on Peachtree in the Flatiron Building. Worth withdrew the cash to pay Frank for the smaller ring. Outside the bank, Worth introduced Frank to Max Abelson, who ran a jewelry and loan business on Forsyth Street. Abelson examined the larger stone and offered $300. Frank was again disappointed but, Worth counseled him to take the money because there'd be more where that came from. He told him, "I can sell whatever you bring me." Frank grudgingly took his $300, presumably a portion of which went to Worth for "services rendered."

Frank DuPre. *Detroit Police photo.*

Frank decided he now needed a gun. He paid seventeen dollars for an automatic pistol at Green's Money to Loan, one of the numerous pawnshops on Decatur Street, near Five Points. He selected a .32 Colt automatic, designed to be concealed in the carrier's pocket. It was said to be "hammerless," but actually the hammer fit within a slide, allowing the weapon to be pulled from a pocket quickly without fear of snagging. It was the "best and safest pocket pistol made."[15] The .32 Colt was the lethal handgun of choice for Sacco and Vanzetti, Dillinger, Capone, Bonnie and Clyde and now Frank DuPre.

When Frank made the decision to arm himself, it was more out of a concern for his personal safety than any plans to shoot up the city. He was carrying lots of cash and mingling in a culture where fights and robberies were not uncommon. He wasn't the biggest fellow in the world, and knowing that he had a pocket pistol at hand was probably greatly reassuring. With a "gat," he was a man to be reckoned with. Frank soon ran into Jack Worth again, who reminded him of his standing offer. Worth suggested that a gutsy fellow could make a lot of money a lot faster by simply smashing windows and taking a whole tray full of rings. Worth may have even taken Frank "window shopping." But Frank figured that kind of job was too dangerous. The Davis & Freeman snatch job had gone off smoothly enough. He would stick to that.

Frank was now staying at the Childs Hotel on South Broad Street, south of the tracks, with a glaring three-story red vertical sign that read "CHILDS HOTEL" (flashing or not). It was a dodgy place, frequently raided by vice agents for liquor and prostitution. But it was affordable; rooms with a bath were two dollars a night. Meals were included on the European plan, and ladies were offered a private dining room.

On December 9, Frank heard the sound of a piano being played from the hotel's mezzanine. Investigating, he found a young lady at the keyboard. Betty Andrews, whose life story and memories of her whirlwind relationship with Frank were to prove to be remarkably changeable, recalled that when she finished playing, Frank spoke to her. "You sure do play fine," he said. She thanked him for the compliment. He asked her where she learned to play so well, and she told him that she was a showgirl. She had been in the touring cast of the racy musical *Chu Chin Chow*, which had just closed a sold-out run at the Atlanta Theatre. Based on the legend of Ali Baba, and featuring a scantily clad dancing harem, folks wondered how Atlanta audiences would receive the play. They loved it. But when the company moved on, Betty stayed behind.

Frank asked her if she would like to go to the pictures. They went to the nearby Alamo No. 2 to see *The Sting of the Lash*, starring Pauline Frederick.

The first date went well, and Betty thought Frank was very nice. He didn't drink, and he didn't swear. He was shy and pretty much silent. They walked out a few more times, got a meal and saw more pictures. Betty was to remain insistent that they did not stay in the same room; she had room 306, and he had room 211. Whatever their sleeping arrangements, Frank plighted his troth to Betty by buying her a dress, a pair of shoes and other pretty accessories. She never asked where he'd gotten the money since he apparently had no job. "When you're stuck on a guy," she smiled, "you don't ask." As the romance gathered pace, the Davis & Freeman money was dwindling. In some dreamier moment, the talk turned to marriage. Betty was clear: if Frank wished to court her, she would have to have nice things. Frank said all she would ever have to do was ask. Betty then made the immortal admission. Betty told DuPre, "Baby, I'd love a diamond ring."

Chapter 4

"Through Mountain Fastnesses"

On the afternoon of December 15, 1921, a diamond ring in his topcoat pocket, Frank returned to the Childs Hotel. Now here was the conundrum. The narrative of the story and song (see Chapter 15) is that Betty wanted a diamond ring, perhaps this exact one, and Frank vowed to get it for her. He went to Kaiser's expecting to repeat the snatch-and-run strategy he had employed twelve days before at Davis & Freeman's. But this time there was trouble. In a panic, he shot down two men in what the papers called "a shower of lead." Even Frank had to realize the ring would have to be hocked to finance their escape for a new life somewhere else.

Frank changed clothes in his room. He then found Betty, bringing her the very ring she desired. But he told her at what cost. He was pretty shaken up, and they cried together. He admitted to being "drunker than I've ever been." She gave him lots of coffee, but Frank had to eat something. He went out to the White Lily Cafeteria on Peachtree for a baked apple and a glass of milk. Refreshed, Frank went in search of Jack Worth.

He found him at the Strand Theatre, only four blocks north of Kaiser's. Frank told him that he had pulled the Kaiser's job. Worth knew of the robbery, of course, as all Atlanta was buzzing with the news. Jack whispered softly, "I'll say one thing, Frank. That sure took some guts." Worth knew he couldn't hock the ring in Atlanta. By law, if not in practice, pawnbrokers had to provide the police with "a full and complete list each day of every article taken in pawn…giving a full description of same." Certainly that didn't keep all pawnbrokers from dealing in some stolen property, but no reasonable broker would get mixed up in a murder case. The ring would have to be "soaked" elsewhere.

Worth, with Frank in tow, went back to Max Abelson for advice. This was quite a different matter from the Davis & Freeman job. Did they tell Abelson the truth? Tellingly, Abelson wanted no part of this deal but suggested that his uncle in Chattanooga might be willing to look at the ring. He provided the address.

There were frequent trains to Chattanooga; a local left at 5:15 p.m. from Union Depot. But that was too risky. The police and "railroad bulls" were watching all trains. The resourceful Worth gave Frank $9 to check out of the Childs. Frank saw Betty and instructed her to check out as well and then wait at the Cecil Hotel. Per Worth's instructions, Frank returned to the Strand and sat in the dark (watching *Lone Star Ranger*, starring William Farnum). At 4:00 p.m., he went to the Rialto Theatre on Forsyth Street, where Worth introduced him to Clifford Buckley, a driver for Belle Isle's taxi service. Buckley drove a powerful Packard twin-six certainly capable of making the run through the mountains. The train fare to Chattanooga would have been $5. Buckley wanted $100. Frank offered $75, and they settled on $90. Frank would pay Buckley out of whatever cash the Tennessee pawnbroker would loan him on the ring.

All these meetings were blithely taking place just blocks from Kaiser's. Police were everywhere. With his ride waiting, Frank went to find Betty, but she wasn't at the Cecil. He reached her by phone still at the Childs; she told him she wouldn't leave without her sister, who couldn't be found. Besides, this was so sudden. Maybe when Frank got settled, he could send her the train fare and then she would join him. While the "lovers" quibbled, Buckley was getting anxious; it was sundown, and the road north was not entirely paved. Frank agreed that Betty could stay behind. He went off clutching the diamond ring he had killed to get for her.

First, however, Worth wanted to try one more local broker. George Wiley's loan company was located above Kaiser's in the Peters Building. Wiley met Worth at West Peachtree and Tenth. He got into Buckley's car, but once Wiley discovered (or so he insisted) that this was "the Kaiser ring," he exploded. He wanted nothing to do with it. Wiley and Worth both got out and went their separate ways, no doubt with Wiley's curses raining down. At 6:00 p.m., with his lone passenger, Buckley steered his Packard out Marietta Street.[16]

The Packard twin-six (V-12), as the salesmen at the dealership on Peachtree would tell you, was the best car in the world. "Ask the man who owns one." The Packard had the stamina, the fuel economy and the pneumatic tires that would be "just adequate" for such a rugged journey.[17] The route to Tennessee followed the northbound trail of the Dixie Highway, a work in progress designed for traffic from the great midwestern cities south through Chattanooga, Atlanta and on to booming Florida.[18] The ride from Atlanta to Chattanooga over the mountains was supposedly a trip of "unending and infinitely varied interest and scenic attraction, a route par excellence for the realization of the joys of motoring."[19] Maybe on another occasion.

Out Marietta Street, the road paralleled the trolley line running to Cobb County. A bridge spanned the Chattahoochee at the hamlet of Bolton. After an hour, Buckley reached Cartersville in Bartow County, where he had a choice: either turn northwest for Rome or northeast to Dalton. Buckley turned for Rome. The *Constitution* had recently sent a reporter, in a similar "sturdy Packard," to test both routes, and Rome was the better road. Motorists were advised to check the daily report of the Highways Weather Bureau Service. That day's forecast predicted good conditions. The night was clear, and the moon was full.

Buckley was told to take his time; he should not drive so fast as to run off the road or, worse, attract the attention of any lawmen out looking for shine runners. The highway had already been christened the "Alcohol Trail." Buckley obeyed; for all he knew, he had a trigger-happy passenger. This man had killed once that day. Buckley was also expecting ninety dollars.

Beyond Rome, the roadway wound higher through "mountain fastnesses" and crossroad villages like Armuchee, Carl and Summerville. There were "several bad curves" and small creeks that might have to be forded. But the road, with chain gang labor, was much improved. The climb up Taylor's Ridge in Chattooga County could now be made "all the way on high gear." On through the December night and early morning, Buckley drove his dozing passenger through Trion, Wilson, Lafayette, Warren Station, Noble and Rock Springs until they reached the Civil War battlefield at Chickamauga. A gravel road crossed the National Military Park, and Buckley would look for the tall granite monument to the Iowa regiment atop Missionary Ridge. The memorial was "inclining to the right." Just beyond was the turn for Rossville. Soon the Tennessee line and the lights of Chattanooga were ahead. The newly paved Rossville Boulevard—a boon to "the man in a hurry"—ran downhill into the center of the city. After a journey of 120 miles, they arrived at 4:00 a.m.

They were early. The shop opened at 7:00 a.m. Star Loans was on East Ninth Street, a street the locals called the "Big Nine."[20] It was the commercial and cultural hub for black Chattanoogans. Blues legend Bessie Smith grew up there. East Ninth was lined with chicken shacks, "store front cathedrals," poolrooms and many pawnshops. Buckley and DuPre, two young white men, sat in the car, keeping as warm as they could. At 7:00, with Buckley, Frank DuPre approached the sign of the three balls at 13 East Ninth Street. They were let in by "old man Silverman." Max Silverman was in his sixties, a native of Russia and an experienced pawnbroker. The bearer of this obviously valuable ring gave his name as "John Doe." Seriously? What did Silverman think he was getting into? The robbery in Atlanta had occurred only eighteen hours prior to DuPre's arrival in Chattanooga. Wouldn't Abelson have telephoned or wired his uncle? Given the circumstances, a heads-up would seem essential. Still, it is possible that Max Silverman had no knowledge of the dead Pinkerton man. If he had looked at his morning edition of the *Chattanooga Daily Times*, there was no mention of it. Nevertheless, the legendary London magistrate Sir John Fielding advised pawnbrokers to be wary: "I am sure that it would be unnecessary to tell them that when a shoe-black brings a diamond ring to pawn, there is great reason to suspect he did not come by it honestly."[21] In Silverman's defense, while he may have certainly thought the ring was hot, there is no certainty that he knew that the thief had killed a man to get it.

The Kaiser's ring had a retail value of $2,500. DuPre had dealt with a pawnbroker before, so he knew he would never get anything approaching that figure. Typically, a pawnbroker will offer one-fourth to one-third of an item's value.[22] The better the stone, the better the offer. (Here I wish to thank Wendy Woloson, the author of *In Hock: Pawning in America from Independence through the Great Depression*, for her assistance in all matters of the pawning profession.) Silverman used his "jeweler's eye" to examine the ring. His own appraisal, not the Kaiser's price tag, meant all. The pawnbroker recognized the ring's value, but given the investment required, he would need to consult his son, who was expected shortly. In the meantime, he sent Frank and Buckley off for breakfast.

The typical urban pawnbroker dealt in watches, silverware and personal items easily hocked, redeemed with interest and maybe hocked again numerous times. To handle this ring, the Silvermans would have to lay out a lot of money and assume a great risk, given the almost certainty that the ring was stolen. Woloson explains that pawnbrokers, above all, have to ensure that they can recoup their investment, i.e., whatever money they decide to offer. To the pawnbroker, the question is always: "How much is this ring worth to me if I end up owning it?" To the customer, the money offered is a loan. In Frank's case, he would leave with cash and a pawn ticket. To get the ring back, he would have to repay the money, plus interest. But the Silvermans had to consider the very likely prospect that they would never see this fellow again. In that case, they would be out their money as well as lost interest—plus they would be stuck with the ring. Yes, it was an extremely valuable ring, but to resell it would mean more expenses. Could they sell it? $2,500 rings weren't in many shop windows on the Big Nine. While Frank and Buckley ate down the street, Max and Abby Silverman palavered and arrived at the figure of $495 as their best offer.

Frank was not happy. He had not come that far for so little; he wanted $700. The negotiations were tense; the longer Frank hung about, the greater the danger. At one point, Silverman shooed the Atlantans into a back room. A Chattanooga detective was approaching on his morning rounds. The policeman saw nothing amiss and plodded off in search of the usual troublemakers. (Detective Sturdivant of Atlanta wondered why his Chattanooga counterpart had not noticed Buckley's car, with black-on-white GA 21 plates, markedly different from the black-on-orange TENN 21 plate.) Frank, no doubt shaken at the sight of the law, reluctantly came down on his request; he would take $600. The Silvermans were firm. They couldn't get that much cash at such an early hour. They proposed to give Frank $400 cash for the ring, and in the event he was unable to redeem the ring, he could return the pawn ticket by registered mail. Doing that meant that he surrendered the ring to Silverman, who would then send him an additional $200. All he had to do was tell them where to wire the money. On this, hands were shaken, and the deal was done.

Clearly, this wasn't a particularly favorable deal for the daring bandit. Yet he was in no place to storm out the door amidst recriminations. The money, hastily cobbled together, exchanged hands. Old man Silverman was handed the ring. Frank got his pawn ticket and his cash. DuPre paid off the faithful Buckley, giving him almost 25 percent of the money he'd just received. To do that, they had to find a store willing to break a $100 bill. Abby, who had gone along with them, turned to Frank and bluntly asked, "So, are you the Atlanta robber?" Frank admitted it. Buckley then drove Frank to Chattanooga's Terminal Station for a northbound Southern Rail train leaving at 10:45 a.m. His well-compensated mission done, Buckley headed the big Packard for home. He knew he was in big trouble.

Alvin Belle Isle was a well-known character who laid claim to being the city's first motorized taxicab driver. He was Atlanta's semiofficial chauffeur, driving celebrity visitors around town. On the night of the shooting, he reported to police that one of his vehicles and the driver were missing. Clifford Buckley had not been seen since about 5:00 p.m. on Thursday. Buckley drove a powerful long-distance Packard. It isn't likely that police immediately connected the missing car with the missing bandit. Long nighttime rides were not unusual. The Belle Isle garage regularly hired out its Packards for "moonlight picnics" and sightseeing. But this was December. Such fast and powerful cars were frequently stolen for joy rides or for moonshine runs. A "stop and detain" lookout was put out for the missing Packard.

Retracing his drive through the mountains, Buckley stopped in Rome and found a telephone. He told Belle Isle that he'd taken a single fare to Chattanooga. The man was in a great hurry and thus hadn't called in before leaving. Belle Isle informed the police that his prodigal driver had been found. But this news of a man "in a great hurry" raised suspicions. Buckley's taxicab was met in Marietta. In a backseat side pocket, police found a recently fired .32 Colt automatic with one shell still chambered.

Buckley was taken to police headquarters on Decatur Street, where he protested that he knew absolutely nothing about the Kaiser's holdup. He had spent Thursday afternoon at the pictures until reporting for work. He'd been waiting at Belle Isle's taxi stand when "someone tapped me on the arm" to say a man needed a taxi from the Railroad YMCA. Driving there, he found a man, a stranger, who needed to get to Chattanooga immediately. The man had no money but said he was going to a pawnshop in that city for a transaction that would pay him well. Buckley priced the fare high: $100. They settled on $90. Knowing that Belle Isle would never approve but wanting the money for Christmas, Buckley took the job. The stranger didn't say much but read one of the afternoon papers, acting as "cool as a cucumber." The fellow then pulled his grey overcoat up and went to sleep for the long drive through the mountains.

Belle Isle fired Buckley on the spot. The police didn't buy his story either, and they held him as an accessory after the fact. The *Constitution*, the most tireless arraigner of the Atlanta police, reported that while police were watching all the trains and scouring the usual criminal dens, the killer had craftily slipped away. The police had failed to alert the city's taxi owners. The mocking headline Saturday morning read, "KILLER-SUSPECT SLUMBERS WHILE OFFICERS SEARCH." Meanwhile, the city council added $1,000 to the reward fund, with the provision that the killer be taken "dead or alive."

Chapter 5

"I'll Blow You Back to Atlanta If You Move"

A tlanta detective T.O. Sturdivant[23] and Fenn, the Pinkerton man, took the next train to Chattanooga, the hapless Buckley in tow. At the Star Loan Company, Chattanooga police chief William Hackett was waiting with Max Silverman. Hackett told the Atlanta lawmen that DuPre had taken a northbound train the previous morning. Kaiser's Paul Bonebrake was present to identify the ring, which Sturdivant pocketed as evidence. Silverman was closely questioned about young "John Doe." The pawnbroker insisted he had no knowledge of the Atlanta robbery. To him, it was a routine transaction, and he explained the arrangement made. Hackett instructed Silverman to let them know immediately should Mr. Doe get in touch. The *Chattanooga Times* reported that a desperate killer had quietly slipped through the city. "Never before has Atlanta been the scene of a crime so daring."

While the investigators were in Tennessee, a Western Union messenger arrived at Belle Isle's Luckie Street garage in Atlanta with a wire for Buckley. Belle Isle signed for the telegram and read it. It was plain that the sender was the "Greycoat Bandit." He had wired Buckley instructions to get word to a woman named Betty Andrews at Childs Hotel. Buckley was to give Betty the enclosed forty-dollar money order for train fare to Norfolk. Buckley should send him a return wire to let him know Betty's plans. With seemingly half the detective force off to Chattanooga, Belle Isle headed for police headquarters.

The cops swooped down on the Childs Hotel. The desk clerk admitted Betty Andrews stayed there but informed police that she was out. Of late, she had a particular male friend, but he had checked out Thursday, about an hour after the shooting. That man had registered as Frank DuPre of Charleston. A bellman said DuPre seemed to be "a swell" with lots of cash. In Betty's room, detectives found a photograph of a man whom the clerk said was surely Frank DuPre. The photo was taken to Kaiser's, where the keen-eyed Drukenmiller positively identified the man as the gunman who'd killed Walker forty-eight hours prior. The Sunday papers named the wanted man for the first time: Frank DuPre.

That Saturday evening, detectives met with Betty Andrews. She knew Frank; they had met about a week ago. But she knew no more about the crime than what was in the papers. He was a nice young man, and she was shocked he had anything to do with that awful shooting. They went to the pictures and had a meal or two, but no more than that. She huffed that it was presumptuous of him to want her to go as far away as Norfolk. She would not have done it. The detectives told her that should she hear from her departed beau, they would appreciate the tip. The police, for the time being, withheld her name from the papers.

Norfolk police were notified and given a description of the bandit. Frank, of course, was expecting a reply from Buckley, and the Western Union office was under surveillance. But Frank's luck had not yet run out. He explained in a letter to Betty that arrived on December 20:

Dear Betty,

Well, a few lines to tell you I am still free and hope to remain that way. I am sorry that you could not leave with me. I got to Chattanooga ok and disposed of the ring there. Only got $300 for it. Believe me, Betty, I sure did risk my life trying to wire you some money from here. I wired $40 to CR Buckley, the fellow that drove me to Chattanooga, and also sent him a message telling him to give you this money and to wire me care of the Western Union here what time you left Atlanta. I think the cops in Atlanta must have gotten my message before he did because when I went to get his answer, there was two detectives waiting for me. I owe my life to the girl clerk in the Western Union office. She put me wise, and it sure was fine of her to do it. I think she fell pretty hard for me. Anyway, I lost $40. Well, Betty, I guess you think I am pretty bad, but if it had not been for that whiskey I would have not done all of that shooting. I would not harm a cat when I am sober and hope you will believe me. Let me know what you are going to do and how much money you will need—make it as little as possible. For God's sake, keep all of this to yourself and please destroy this

*letter. Please excuse all these mistakes as I am a little nervous today. Hoping
to hear from you soon, I remain,
Your lover, Frank.*

Betty would have disappointed her ardent correspondent had he known
that she took this letter to Atlanta's chief of detectives, Lamar Poole.
Sturdivant and Fenn were back on a train for Norfolk with Betty Andrews,
the human lure they hoped to use to ensnare the Peachtree Bandit. Poole,
without revealing the source for his optimism, assured the *Constitution* that
"we are on the right track and will clear up this case very soon."

Meanwhile, Frank was now in the frame for several more crimes. Clerks
at three other Atlanta jewelers claimed to recognize him from the police
photograph. Davis & Freeman's Raymond Tooke was certain DuPre
had stolen two rings from their store on December 3. Two more jewelers
claimed to recognize the squint-eyed youth who'd stolen rings back into
the summer. Since Frank insisted that he never stole a thing until he
pinched the money from Reville in early November, the new claims may
be dubious. Of course, police were known to clear up as many cases as
they could if given the opportunity.

In his jail cell, Clifford Buckley also identified the man as his sleeping
passenger. But the Norfolk telegram had clearly put Buckley in a tighter spot.
That DuPre would trust him with word of his hideout and send him forty
dollars indicated a much closer tie than a simple driver-fare relationship.
Detectives thought it was beyond time that Buckley be more candid. As these
things often work out, Buckley was soon "freely talking."

Buckley now told the police that on Thursday afternoon, he'd been to
see *The Immaculate Irish Gentleman* with Robert Reilly at the Lyric Theatre. At
four o'clock, as he walked up Carnegie Way, he ran into a fellow he knew
named Jack Worth, who had another man with him. Worth said, "Here is
the man that pulled that job." Worth asked if Buckley would drive DuPre
to Chattanooga, where there was a pawnbroker who would "soak" the ring.
Once DuPre got his cash, Buckley would get $75. Buckley demanded $100.
He knew Belle Isle would never allow him to take the car overnight, but the
money would be handy for Christmas. "I work on commission, and such
a big fare meant a right good sum for me." They agreed on $90. Before
leaving Atlanta, however, Worth set up a meeting with George Wiley, but
Wiley angrily refused to deal with the ring. By then, it was already dark, and
Buckley said they left for Chattanooga at 6:00 p.m. DuPre didn't say much.
He bought a newspaper; the headlines were all about the shooting. Buckley

heard the fellow say that it was a "terrible" thing. Buckley swore that as soon as he got paid, he headed south. By now, the police had determined the gun found in the Packard was the murder weapon, but Buckley insisted that he never saw a gun.

On Wednesday, December 21, police arrested Jack Worth and George Wiley. Worth was picked up at Cooper & Towery's barbershop and pool hall on Peachtree. The papers reported that Worth worked there, but the management demanded a retraction, stating that he only hung out there. The cops even took a ring off Mrs. Worth's finger but later returned it when they couldn't prove it had been stolen. Wiley was arrested at his office in the Peters Building. By Friday, Buckley, Worth and Wiley were indicted as accessories after the fact and held incommunicado. The *Constitution* declared, "DEEPEST MYSTERY SHROUDS ACTIONS OF CITY SLEUTHS." Wiley posted bond, however, and told reporters all he knew. He had gone to meet Worth about a ring, but once he learned it was from the Kaiser's job, he shouted, "Let me out of here!" It was a bad business. He had never seen the bandit before or since. Still, Wiley admitted that he had not gone to the police.

By Christmas, the police were still confident. Worth, Wiley and Buckley had been rolled up. The detectives, with Betty as bait, spent their holiday up in Tidewater country. Every day, it seemed, the police were "this close" to nabbing the bandit. The *Journal* reported that the "net spread to catch the Peachtree Street bandit was fast growing tight." The following day, the *Constitution* advised their readers that DuPre's arrest was "only a matter of time."

Yet days passed, and the Peachtree Bandit remained at large. After leaving Chattanooga, Frank had taken the Southern Railway, changing in Roanoke to the Norfolk and Western line. The N&W's busy tracks brought coal from Appalachia to fuel the ships of the world's leading navy. Frank knew Norfolk somewhat from his brief stint in the navy. When he arrived on the Saturday after the shooting, he went to the posh Monticello Hotel on Grandy Street, registering as F.B. Parker. After settling in, he sent the wire to Buckley with the forty dollars for Betty from the Western Union office on East Main Street.

The next day, after catching the silent film *Salvation Nell*, Frank returned to the Norfolk station to ask for his telegrams. There, he got that timely warning from the girl in the Western Union office. "Scram, quick," she whispered. Frank knew that the police were on his heels. In his letter to Betty, he confessed to being nervous. He did not know that Betty was now assisting his pursuers. Sturdivant, Fenn and Betty had arrived by train in Norfolk on

Monday. The cops had sent wires—under Betty's name, of course—letting Frank know that she was in Norfolk and that she would meet him anywhere. But Frank, having already been spooked once, was too scared to go back to the telegraph office. Meanwhile, Pinkerton agents trolled the limitless criminal hangouts of Norfolk, "the East Coast's Sin Capital, the wickedest of port towns." The elusive shooter was not to be found.

After two nights at the Monticello, Frank moved to cheaper lodgings. He spent his days mostly at the movies. He read the papers. He learned that the police believed the bandit had gone to Norfolk to rejoin the navy or maybe hire on a commercial ship. The seaport city was being "scoured." Frank couldn't risk staying there much longer. He could have gone most any direction by train from Norfolk. On Wednesday, December 21, he took an N&W train for Detroit. Why Detroit? Police later surmised he hoped to flee to Canada. In Detroit, he could have easily taken a ferry or even walked across the frozen Detroit River to Ontario. (There was no bridge until 1929.) However, Canada did not guarantee freedom; the U.S.-Canada extradition treaty for murder was long established. Frank went to Detroit, very likely, because it was as far as he could go to elude his pursuers.

Frank's slip to Detroit went undiscovered. In Atlanta, with each day's disappointment, the pressure built on the police. The crime wave had not abated. In late December, a newsboy's throat was slashed at Broad and Marietta Streets; two people were shot dead in the West End, while a team of "bicycle burglars" had ransacked the new upscale Peachtree Hills neighborhood. It was so bad that "Colonel" W.J. Simmons, the Atlanta man who headed the reborn Georgia Klan, offered hundreds of armed Klansmen to patrol the city.

On December 29, under the headline "IN THE GRIP OF CRIME," the *Constitution* declared, "And so it goes, night after night, day after day, killings, shooting, bludgeoning. Stick-ups, highway robberies, burglaries, pilfering, and petty thievery of every description going on in all parts of the city—and the condition has reached the point where no man's life is safe even in his own home, let alone in his place of business or on the street!" A furious Mayor Key went to the friendlier editors at the *Journal* to accuse the morning paper of "grossly exaggerated and highly libelous statements" about Atlanta. He called it a "trail of slime." The city would hire one hundred more policemen immediately. In the meantime, the relentless *Constitution* jibed that the daring Peachtree Bandit "still enjoys his freedom."

The calendar changed to 1922, and on January 3, the police shamefacedly admitted that the trail was lost in Norfolk and quietly returned home. Their

Norfolk brethren had arrested the whistle-blowing Western Union clerk. But three weeks after the deadly shooting, Atlanta police were at a loss. In 1920s newspaper crime jargon, the sleuths had few "clews" in their hunt for the Peachtree Bandit.

What must young DuPre have thought as he read those papers in his Detroit room? The *Georgian* compared his daring raid and deft escape to "great Confederate generals like Forrest." He read of the "brazen bandit" who had outsmarted the police. What a thrill to be called a "desperado." He was such a cool customer. It was the work of an accomplished professional. He was always a step ahead of the law. He was so clever to take a cab. They had just missed him in Chattanooga. They missed him in Norfolk. He was being hunted like a ravening dog. He was such a dangerous fellow that the cops had been given a see-him-and-shoot-him edict. But while pursued by every means known to detective science, he had fooled them all. No wonder he got the idea that the police were all "boneheads." But what a fatal mistake it was to write it down.

On the evening of January 12, a messenger brought a special-delivery envelope, postmarked in Atlanta, to the offices of the *Constitution* on Alabama Street. Inside was a letter, written with a fountain pen on quality pad paper. The three-hundred-word letter was boldly signed, THE PEACHTREE BANDIT. It had to be verified. A bank executive, said to be Atlanta's foremost handwriting expert, was consulted. At the Childs, the letter was matched with DuPre's signature on the desk registry, the only known example of his handwriting. The banker was certain that both documents had been written by the same person. The letter appeared in the *Constitution*'s morning edition of Friday, January 13, 1922:

Dear Sir,

I wrote you a letter some time ago, and I don't think you received it as it has not been published. I would like to say that I think Atlanta has a bunch of boneheads for detectives. They don't seem to be able to catch anybody. I gave them several chances to get me and they have failed so far. I went to the expense of sending them a telegram which cost me close to $45 including the money I wired for my girlfriend. Thanks to Mr. Belle Isle they got the message. I will try to repay him later for this favor. I believe Mr. Poole stated I was in hiding. Well, he is badly mistaken. I am not in hiding and don't intend to be. About Buckley—I never saw him before the night he took me to Chattanooga. He did not know I was a bandit, and *what would any taxi driver do if he had a chance of taking a passenger to Chattanooga? As for those other two fellows indicted in the case, I have never had the pleasure of meeting them and have not the least idea who they are. I almost forgot Mr. West, sorry I had to shoot him but he insisted on stopping me. And there was no other way out of it. I think he will mind his own business hereafter, which will be much better for him if he does. Thank you in advance. I remain yours truly, "THE PEACHTREE BANDIT." P.S.—my age is 19.*

The tradition of criminals writing such taunting catch-me-if-you-can letters to the police is a long-standing one. Undoubtedly the most famous was the "Dear Boss" note sent to Scotland Yard in 1888, supposedly by Jack the Ripper. The tone is strikingly similar to Frank's letter: "I keep on hearing the police have caught me, but they wont fix me just yet. I have laughed when they look so clever and talk about being on the right track." The tradition continues today: New York's Son of Sam, San Francisco's Zodiac Killer and, in 2004, the D.C. snipers. Jack Levin, a criminologist at Boston's Northeastern University, suggests such letters "are designed to maximize the killer's feeling of power, superiority, relative to the community and the police."[24] Others think the letters arise more from a need for continuing notoriety; when the story goes cold, the hunted man wants to remind everyone that he's still out there.

Atlanta had its own recent history in this area, a history of which Frank would have been aware. In 1921, Floyd Woodward, indicted by Solicitor Boykin as the head of the city's bunco ring, disappeared before he could be arrested. Days later, Woodward sent a mocking letter accusing Boykin of taking bribes from the syndicate. Woodward remained free until 1940. Also in 1921, stockbroker and socialite R.N. Berrien disappeared shortly before a teacher's bond fund that he managed collapsed. Berrien wrote directly to Governor Hardwick to say he had no intention of being captured but that if granted amnesty, he would return and work to restore the lost monies. Berrien was arrested in New York City and later imprisoned.

The Atlanta police were skeptical. Poole examined the letter under a high-powered magnifying glass and concluded the idea that DuPre had written it was "absolutely ridiculous." This was someone's effort to embarrass the Atlanta police department. It was probably written by some friend of Worth or Wiley. "It doesn't take a boneheaded detective to know that the letter is propaganda," scoffed Chief of Detectives Poole.

Meanwhile, another letter from Frank DuPre had been delivered. In Detroit, Frank was living in a dingy rooming house and was down to his last $4. On January 12, he sent a registered letter to Max Silverman in Chattanooga enclosing the pawn ticket for the ring in hock. Under their agreement, Frank surrendered all claim to the ring and, in return, expected $200 from Silverman. Frank requested that the money be wired to "F.B. Parker, c/o General Delivery at the main Detroit Post Office." Silverman immediately contacted Chief Hackett. Detroit police were notified.

What was DuPre thinking? If, as reported, Frank was avidly reading all the papers, how did he miss the fact that Silverman no longer had the ring? It was in a police safe in Atlanta. That information was not kept from the press. By returning the now-useless pawn ticket to Chattanooga, Frank DuPre stamped his own ticket for death row.

The main post office and federal building in Detroit and its 240-foot clock tower was a landmark. The marble-clad lobby was a "hell of a place to buy a 2-cent stamp."[25] Frank DuPre approached the building on the evening of Friday the thirteenth. Five well-armed Detroit plainclothesmen were in position. They had seen DuPre's photo, and when a young man approached "ambling aimlessly," he was recognized immediately. First to grab him were Detectives William Collins and Paul Wenzel. With guns drawn, they jumped DuPre in a crowd while others quickly pinned his arms. More cops rushed in from all directions. The *Detroit Free Press* reported that an understandable panic ensued on the busy sidewalk. A detective yelled, "I'll blow you back to Atlanta if you move." Frank surrendered meekly. He was unarmed. The Peachtree Bandit was in custody.

This being the Motor City, Frank was bundled into a powerful "detective flyer" for the drive to the Central Station on Randolph Street. There, Frank later told an Atlanta reporter that he had been given "the third degree." In a room with one bright light shining in his eyes, he could not see his interrogators. He was questioned by Detroit's chief of detectives, Edward Fox. Perhaps Fox pulled out his pocket watch to mark the time of the interview—the watch that would, weeks later, stop a bullet and save his life when he walked in on a robbery in progress. Fox told Frank that whatever he said would be taken down and used against him at a trial. Frank replied, "I might as well tell you all about it." Chain-smoking cigarettes, he opened up.

It was this first confession that launched the legend of Betty Andrews. To this point, Betty was known only to the police as Frank's short-time girlfriend. That would all end after headlines such as "DUPRE SAYS HE STOLE FOR SHOW GIRL" were printed. Frank said he had known Betty for about a week. They had walked out to a few movies and had also done some window-shopping downtown. They passed by Kaiser's, where she told him how much she liked a particular ring. Betty was not just another girl, Frank bragged. "She was with the *Chu Chin Chow* show, and she told me I would have to get some money if I wanted to go with her, so I went out after the diamond we had noticed in the store." He had bought the gun on December 5. At about noon on December 15, before setting out for Kaiser's, he bought some moonshine and went back to Betty's room, where they "killed the bottle." He told the Detroit police, "Betty persuaded me to do it. She loved pretty things and, well, I got them for her." Once in the store, with the diamond in his hand, he turned to run. "Walker was standing near the door, and when I started to run out, he blocked the way, pushing me halfway back thru the store and reaching for his gun. I had the automatic in my coat pocket, and when it was on level with his heart, I pulled the trigger twice."

According to Frank, he blacked out, and next thing he knew he was back in his hotel room. An hour or so later, he sought out Jack Worth, who hooked him up with Buckley. They drove all night along bad roads to Chattanooga. He had threatened to shoot Buckley if he went too fast and attracted the police. Silverman didn't see them until sunrise. With the money from the ring, he left that morning for Norfolk, where he stayed only a week. He got to Detroit a few days before Christmas, but without a job or money, he decided to return the ticket to Silverman and had gone to the post office to get his $200. The detectives reported that Frank seemed pretty bitter, accusing Silverman of betraying him. Otherwise, he seemed resigned to his fate. He was tired of running and was willing to go back to Atlanta and "face the music." He even asked the Detroit police if they knew whether Georgia used the rope or the chair. "All I want is a fair deal," he said.

Chapter 6

"Anything Less Than Death"

Atlanta's tireless newsboys were out early Saturday shouting word of the arrest. It was the "lone topic for conversation." Meanwhile, police and reporters headed for Detroit. Extradition papers had been prepared by the governor's office, but DuPre would return without a fight. Solicitor Boykin announced plans for a speedy trial. "Of course, I shall be seeking the death penalty," he said.

When arrested, Frank was carrying a Detroit newspaper open to the society pages. He had circled the names of families reported to be in Florida for the winter. The police thought he planned to burglarize their vacant homes. But in Frank's room on Columbia Avenue, police found no weapons and no valuables other than Reville's pilfered watch. They did find scraps of letters indicating that Frank had tried out several Peachtree Bandit notes. One was signed, "Your friend, the lucky bandit, who has never been caught." In another, Frank chirped, "It's no use to look for me out of Atlanta—I have not left Atlanta, and am, as this is being written, within sight and sound of the Constitution building. The Atlanta Police Department couldn't catch a cold—and you can tell 'em for me that they needn't try to catch me. Because it will be wasting their time to try."

Mayor Key, whose feud with the *Constitution* was white hot, told the *Georgian*, "I am glad that Atlanta's boldest criminal and staff correspondent of the *Constitution* has been caught."

With DuPre in custody, the focus turned to his mysterious girlfriend, the reputed inspiration for one of the most daring crimes in Atlanta history. The

Journal headlined, "DUPRE'S OWN STORY—'I STOLE DIAMOND TO GIVE BETTY.'" At the Childs Hotel, Betty Andrews was besieged by reporters. That evening, she sent out a brief statement: "I did not know Frank was a criminal, and I did not aid him." Sunday morning's *Constitution* presented a more elaborate statement, more the work of a lawyer than that of a teenage girl:

> *He fell in love with me, but it was not my fault and I did nothing to encourage him to do so. God knows I am sorry for the boy, but I cannot make myself feel that I am in any way responsible for his crimes. Any intimation from any source that I encouraged DuPre to steal the diamond is absolutely false. I did not love him, and knowing him only four days, I scarcely felt in a position to aid or influence him in the commission of any crime. I was with him on the streets only one time, and then we went to the theater. I positively never was with him on the streets looking in jewelry windows and admiring rings.*

Betty mania was underway. "She is a pretty little trick, this Betty Andrews. She is stylish, knows how to wear her clothes and fix her hair [but] now with her bandit lover behind bars, she presents the forlornest sort of figure," assessed the *Constitution*'s Fuzzy Woodruff. "She hasn't even the glamour about her of the woman of fiction, who remains steadfast and true to her pal when caught in the net of the law." The *Journal* described her as a pretty girl with a "wealth of golden hair and big blue eyes." The *Georgian* printed the first pictures of Betty. Far from golden-haired, Betty was a brunette with large sad eyes and heavily painted pouty lips of the flapper style. She held court with the reporters in the parlor of her hotel until the management asked her to leave.

Betty's story was that she found herself in Atlanta after quitting the *Chu Chin Chow* company, owing to a weak heart. Taking a room at the Childs, she met Frank four days before the shooting. She had been playing the hotel piano, and he had complimented her. They went to movies and the like, but she denied Frank's story that they'd gone window-shopping for a ring. She had told him that whenever she did get married, she'd want a big diamond. Frank was a shy young man, and she had no idea that he was a jewel thief. The morning of the Kaiser's job, she had seen him in the hotel. He seemed fine and said nothing. That afternoon, he came in acting rather "doped" and wanted her to go with him to Chattanooga. It was too sudden, and she refused. She hadn't seen a paper that day, so she didn't know anything about

FIRST PHOTOS OF BETTY ANDREWS

Betty Andrews. Atlanta Georgian, *January 18, 1922.*

the robbery. "I am awfully sorry for Frank DuPre, but I did not lead him to commit any crime," she said. "I never asked him for a ring or for any money. I have an allowance from my father. I did not tell him that I loved him."

Meanwhile, Atlanta's contingent of press and police reached Detroit late on Sunday. Sturdivant went directly to the jail, taking down Frank's second confession, which differed in several ways from the one taken down by the Detroit interrogators. Frank was less specific in his claim that Betty had "persuaded" him to steal the ring. But she had told him that she would have to have a big diamond, and he vowed to get her one. Frank again claimed that he had been so drunk he remembered nothing. But Sturdivant asked why, then, had he thought to change clothes. Frank muttered, "Common sense, I guess." Frank also talked at length about his dealings with Jack Worth and the arrangement for Buckley to drive him to Chattanooga.

Sturdivant wired DuPre's confession back to Atlanta. The papers were now describing Worth as a Fagin-esque leader of a gang of thieves. Worth's attorney, Len Guillebeau, called DuPre's statement "hellish propaganda." Worth roared, "That bird is trying to pass the buck to save his crooked neck." Meanwhile, Buckley was formally charged with having "harbored, concealed and aided" the fugitive bandit. And a new name had surfaced: Vincent Geoghan. The letters found in Frank's Detroit room implicated Geoghan as the man who posted the "boneheads" letter to the *Constitution*. A letter from Geoghan was also found in Frank's room. It read, in part, "Dear Frank, sorry you got in that trouble…You will have to be very careful and not let any woman know your trouble. Do not give up but try to follow the straight road." Geoghan was arrested at the shabby Postal Hotel on Fairlie Street.

On Monday, the Atlanta reporters in Detroit were allowed to see DuPre. His cell floor strewn with cigarette butts, and the bandit had not been sleeping. The *Journal's* Angus Perkerson said DuPre looked sunken and tired. "He looks as little like a bandit as any man. He is much younger than he seems in the pictures. It seemed impossible that the pasty faced boy smoking cigarettes could be the robber who killed Irby Walker." DuPre's only explanation was, "If I didn't know that I was drunk and out of my mind when I did it, I'd go clean crazy." He had been out of work since July and admitted pulling the Davis & Freeman job earlier in December. Worth helped him hock the rings. Then he met Betty, and he fell hard. But she was a girl accustomed to luxury, and she made it clear that to go with her, he would have to get her nice things, like a diamond ring. The *Georgian's* W.E. Willits listened to "the whole sorry story of [DuPre's] life." It was DuPre's infatuation for Betty Andrews that drove him to rob and kill.

Frank was talking freely. Soon he would be headed back to Georgia, where the penalty for murder was the noose. He needed legal assistance. An uncle, James Cox, was the county coroner in Abbeville. He contacted Ben Chappelle, an Atlanta lawyer with Abbeville ties. Chappelle recommended a criminal lawyer named Henry Allen. Nearly forty, lanky and with a thick wave of hair cresting over his left ear, Allen was from Hapeville, south of the city. He was also a rare bird around the courthouse in that he was a Republican.[26] He and Boykin had clashed before when Allen defended a policeman charged with taking bribes from an infamous black bootlegger, Nat McWhorter. He had done murder cases before as well; early in 1921, Allen defended Jack Kelloy, an Atlanta youth accused of killing a cab driver. The victim's body was found on a roadside in Griffin. Kelloy was arrested, tried and sentenced to hang—all in two weeks. Allen's appeals dragged the case out for months until a final claim of insanity was rejected by Governor Hardwick. In July, on gallows built behind the Spalding County Courthouse, Kelloy hanged with "a crucifix clasped in his manacled hands."

Frank's lead defense counsel, Henry A. Allen. *Courtesy of Allen's granddaughter Mrs. Anne Green Westbrook.*

Allen was assisted by two other veteran lawyers: Colonel Izzard Heyward and Louis Foster. They may have had numbers, but they didn't have much time. Boykin was going to get his speedy trial. The grand jury indicted DuPre on Friday. The trial would start on Tuesday. Allen had not even met his client.

On Tuesday morning, January 17, a small motorcade left the Detroit jail, splashing through rainy streets to Michigan Central Station. In the cavernous waiting room, modeled on the Roman baths of Caracalla, commuters and travelers looked up from their papers to see a slight youth, in a cloth coat with a cap pulled down tightly on his head, shuffling past. The observant noted that his hands were cuffed and his legs shackled. Grim-faced policemen flanked the young man. Another small knot of men, reporters from Atlanta, followed. A southbound "Big Four" train left for Cincinnati at 8:00 a.m. Frank DuPre was going south.

With a change of trains in Cincinnati, Atlanta was thirty hours away. Sturdivant assured the newsmen (and other passengers) that DuPre would be under constant watch. But Frank bore little resemblance to a dangerous fugitive killer. The *Georgian* reported that his earlier air of confidence had disappeared: "He left here a weeping boy, nerves shattered and hands trembling from the hundreds of cigarettes he has smoked." The *Journal's* Perkerson reported that DuPre was openly hoping that he wouldn't hang, quoting him as saying, "I'm asking for a chance. I'm asking because I'm just a kid. I'm eighteen, not nineteen, I was drunk, blind drunk. I want just a chance to keep living and in any way I can make up for what's happened."

A Louisville & Nashville train left Cincinnati's Central Union Station, crossing the Ohio River on Tuesday evening for the remaining fourteen-hour trip. Frank ate some fried chicken and ice cream. He slept handcuffed to his berth. The train reached Georgia by sunrise on Wednesday. Frank was taken into the buffet car for breakfast. He had been made presentable for his arrival. Sturdivant had shaved him, and he was carrying the "grey overcoat that had become his nom de plume." While in Cincinnati, word had reached the reporters that DuPre's lawyers were considering an insanity plea. The newsmen encircled Frank's seat. "Are you crazy, Frank?" they asked. He didn't think he was. "Of course, I might be nutty and never know it." But when asked if he thought he were crazy, he answered, "No, I don't." Sturdivant took it all down.

Thirty minutes late, the L&N train steamed in to Atlanta's aging, soot-stained Union Depot. Built in 1871, the structure replaced the one that Sherman put to the torch. On a grey, cold January day, the waiting crowd was one of Atlanta's biggest ever, rivaling the throngs that welcomed the great Caruso or General "Black Jack" Pershing. It was a pickpocket's holiday. The crowd might have even been larger had not the *Constitution* mistakenly reported that DuPre was expected on the Southern Railroad train from Cincinnati, due at the larger Terminal station. Alas, those who gathered there saw nothing but bewildered satchel-toting passengers wondering why so many folks had turned out to greet them.

Meanwhile, at the depot, police struggled to control the crowd. DuPre remained on the train until a path was cleared for a Stutz four-seater touring car, with Chief Beavers, in full enjoyment of the moment, shouting and waving instructions from the running board. The Stutz drew up alongside the Pullman platform, and the man of the day emerged. From the platform, DuPre could have looked up to see the Peters Building, one hundred yards away, with Kaiser's open for business. In front of him was the hulking form of the Kimball House. But he did not look up. Instead, as the *Georgian* reported, the "badly frightened young slayer was watching wild-eyed as a crowd of onlookers pressed against him." A cordon of policemen held the crowd back. It wasn't a vengeful crowd; they pushed and strained to see, but there were few expressions of hostility. Chief of Detectives Poole had boarded the train, and he and Sturdivant practically carried the slighter bandit to the car. The crowd surged in for a closer look, blocking Pryor Street. Police forced them back; a copper bellowed, "Haven't you boobs ever seen a prisoner before?"

The narrowest of paths appeared, and the car roared up Pryor Street, with "men and boys racing headlong behind." It was a memorable ten minutes, wrote the *Constitution*'s Woodruff: "A pale, timorous, mouse-like sort of a man was lifted off a train at the Union Station…His beady, shifting, little eyes turned away from the thousands that were seeking to stare into them. The killer's fangs had been drawn by the law, and all that was left was a fear-torn, sheet-white, nerve-racked body covered by a gray overcoat…so the Peachtree Bandit returned to the scene of his exploit."

The Stutz, heedless of its pursuers, made the four-block run out Decatur Street to police headquarters. DuPre was hustled in through the two-story central archway. Among those he was rushed past was a woman in a black mourning dress. The *Georgian* observed that Gladys Walker evidenced no change of emotion on seeing for the first time the man who had slain her husband.

The booking procedures were followed. A mug shot was taken. It took three tries to get a good set of fingerprints from Frank's clammy, shaking hands. Frank was then was allowed a brief opportunity to meet his lawyers.

Allen had only the chance to introduce himself. He told Frank to get some rest and, above all, stop talking.

Allen had been accompanied to the station by Frank's father and Betty Andrews. Given Frank's claims about Betty's role in this tragedy, the elder DuPre had no reason to be delighted to make her acquaintance. Still, he graciously commented, "We're both working for Frank—we're sure to be the best of friends." The elder DuPre was a small, haggard man who seemed frantic with understandable worry. His first words to his son were, "You are smoking too many cigarettes." Later, he told reporters that Frank had never been in trouble; his late mother had called him "the old man" because he was so refined. DuPre said he never should have left Frank alone in Atlanta. "He is just a boy led to do a terrible thing by older men," he said.

Betty was allowed only the briefest reunion with her erstwhile swain; her words, spoken through wails of tears, were "unintelligible." Betty asked Frank how he was doing, and he replied, "Pretty good considering." Poole cut things off, and DuPre was put in a holding cell with three men, probably delighted to have a chance to tell their mates how they were locked up with the infamous bandit. Frank politely shook their hands and told them, "Well, I'm here to get it over with." That night, he was moved a few blocks east to the Fulton County Jail, commonly referred to as the "Tower."

Built of Stone Mountain granite, the "Big Rock" stood five stories tall. From the rooftop, the eponymous Tower rose another sixty feet. The main building contained four wings surrounding a central arcade. Built in 1898, it was said only half in jest that it was second only to the Kimball House in terms of accommodations. By 1922, it was a hellish place—overcrowded, stench filled and forced to house the county's mentally ill.

The rival lawyers did some preliminary fencing. Allen said his first impression of DuPre was how young he was. He was clearly a thoughtless youth and hardly the brazen bandit the press had created. Would there be an insanity plea? Allen reserved his answer. Solicitor Boykin dismissed talk of the suspect's youth or insanity. "We do not believe a jury will listen to any talk of hereditary insanity," he said. "He robbed a store in broad daylight in the heart of the city and killed an officer who tried to stop him and tried to kill another citizen." The charge was murder. "There will not be the slightest compromise or softening of the prosecution."

John Boykin was forty-five, born in Edgefield, South Carolina. A staff lawyer under former solicitor Hugh Dorsey, he helped prosecute Leo Frank. Boykin later believed the conviction was a "horrible mistake." When Dorsey quit to run (successfully) for governor, Boykin was elected to his first four-year term as solicitor in 1916. He would serve seven terms, boasting that he survived numerous death threats (one of his top investigators was assassinated). When he finally retired in 1944, the Associated Press reported that the underworld had learned one thing: "Steer clear of Atlanta—that's John Boykin's town." He was a large, broad-shouldered man with "sparkling blue eyes." He lived on Myrtle Street in Midtown and was a steward of his church, St. Mark's United Methodist, where his wife was active in the Young Matron's Circle. Boykin relaxed by fishing for mountain trout. We cannot close this potted biography without quoting from the famous book, *I Am a Fugitive from a Georgia Chain Gang*. The author of that supposedly true tale was Robert

A 1920 campaign photograph of Fulton County solicitor general John Boykin. *Author's collection.*

Burns, who crossed paths with Boykin. "[He had] a face in which there was no trace of kindness," wrote Burns. "This was John A. Boykin, the most feared man in the state of Georgia."[27]

While the lawyers postured and Frank sat in a cell, Betty Andrews made more headlines. Her daily interviews were making increasingly less sense. In the *Georgian*, she claimed to have been privately trained in music and dance. Her parents were divorced and lived "up North." In one moment, she enthused that Frank was "a man whom most women would like, even after a short acquaintance," and in the next she offered the opinion that "the insane asylum is the place for him. In my mind, there is no doubt that he is crazy." But she would stand by him. "I would do anything I possibly could for him, although I realize how useless it would be."

Betty talked to Victoria Iler, one of the first female reporters at the *Journal*. Betty gushed, "Isn't he good looking? You're a woman and you know what it means to be in love." Betty promised to attend the trial and vowed that if he were spared, she would marry him in prison. But if he were hanged, she would take poison. Miss Iler noted that Betty's clothes gave an appearance of wealth. "Her modish brown suit trimmed in beaver was matched with a spring hat of the same shade," she wrote. She wore "brown gauntlet shoes, embroidered silk hose and trim brown slippers." Betty insisted that the clothes came from an allowance from her father, who lived up north with her invalid mother.

With Betty's picture appearing daily in the papers in Atlanta and elsewhere, it was not surprising that her narrative would be challenged. The police spoiled the showgirl angle quickly—no one with the *Chu Chin Chow* show had ever heard of her. On the night of January 19, the day after DuPre's return to Atlanta, Betty was brought to Boykin's office. During lengthy questioning, she tearfully admitted that Frank had purchased all the clothes she had on, likely with the money from the Davis & Freeman heist. Her fur-trimmed dress had cost a staggering $65.00, her "jaunty" hat $12.50, her gloves $7.50, her silk hose $3.50 and her "trim brown slippers" another $8.00.

By the morning, the *Constitution*'s headline cried, "BETTY ANDREWS WATCHED DUPRE SNATCH JEWEL AND SHOOT DOWN DETECTIVE ASSERT SLEUTHS." Boykin said they could prove Betty's involvement "beyond peradventure." She had been part of a gang of jewel thieves employed to case likely targets and act as lookouts. Boykin said he could place Betty in the entryway to the Peachtree Arcade, watching from across the street for her lover to emerge with the ring she coveted. Betty, reported the *Georgian*, had "broken down under grilling" and admitted to everything. Badly shaken, her "hitherto jaunty manner" was gone.

The myth of Betty Andrews was shattered in a day's news cycle. She was no showgirl. She had no wealthy parents "up North." She was from Gainesville, the daughter of a churchgoing farmer/house painter named Joseph Guest. Her mother was the grandchild of Cherokee Indians. "Her mother and I rue the day we let her leave the mountains for the bright lights of Atlanta," Mr. Guest moaned. He did deny a *Constitution* report that Betty's mind had been affected by brain fever as a child. Guest declared, "She's not crazy." The most stunning news of all, however, was that Betty was married! Her estranged husband was Earl Anderson, a downtown barber a dozen years older than Betty. They met when he was in the army at Camp Gordon and she was an operator at the Hemlock Exchange on Crescent Street. They married in 1918 but quickly split. Anderson denied that he beat her. "She doesn't know what love is," he said. "She has wrecked my life." The *Constitution*'s Woodruff reported that Betty was known to partake of the "sordid side of the city's night life." The romantic story of a love-struck boy and girl had been made from whole cloth. "It's a pity to spoil the romance. But these are the facts."

On Sunday morning, Frank was taken to the Tower's hospital ward to see Dr. Frank Eskridge. Boykin had to be ready to meet any insanity defense. Eskridge was one of the city's best-known surgeons and had long been interested in the criminal brain. In 1911, Sam Swatson, a Negro about to hang for sexually assaulting a white girl, willed his brain to Eskridge. The doctor believed that "a close examination of the negro's mental apparatus may reveal something which will add to the scientific data accumulated by criminologists and perhaps help to correct a tendency toward crime by operations early in youth."[28]

Frank spent two hours with Eskridge, undergoing a physical examination and conversing on a wide variety of subjects. The doctor refused to discuss his findings with reporters, but his report can be found in the DuPre file later submitted to Governor Hardwick.

Examined him 22 Jan in the hospital ward of the Tower. Physical: Medium stout, 130 pounds, 69 inches. Congenital squint in the left eye that gives a semi ptosis appearance. Bad acne on his back. Has consistency of fecal matter. Had his tonsils out at four or five. Good health but had pneumonia while in the Navy. Started smoking at 15 and now smokes about 60 per day. Claims to have only had two quarts of whiskey in his life. Penis and testicles normal. Never had venereal disease but admits he has had pediculi pubis (crabs). Admits that he has been with bad women.

His emotional health: He enjoyed working at the Film Company and was up to $20 a week when first laid off. He joined the Navy in December 1920 but was discharged March 8, 1921. Returned to Atlanta, loafed, then went back to Scenic but for only $10 a week. Laid off again in July. Stayed in a boarding house until his money ran out. Returned to Abbeville but back to Atlanta around the time of the Southeastern Fair, staying with a relative at Howell Station. One Sunday night, he was standing at Tom Pitts corner, hungry and broke, when the husband of his first cousin came by. He was flush from his job and showed him a roll of $140. He was invited to spend the night at his hotel, and he robbed him and lived off it until the Davis-Freeman job.

Answered questions quickly. Cooperative. Sleeps well now but hadn't been in Detroit. He is rather vindictive to those he says have "double crossed" him, including Betty, but he hopes "she comes out alright." The pawnbroker should be indicted, and he will use every effort to have him as he "squealed" upon him. He states that he never had a sweetheart; never cared for girls except those of immoral character. Denies sexual perversion. States that he is normal in habits. Denies any delusions or hallucinations. He knew who was the mayor, the governor, and the meaning of July 4th, etc.

From the foregoing mental and physical examination, it is my professional opinion that Frank DuPre is not suffering from any form of insanity. The fact that he passed the 8th grade in school and entered the Navy shows that he is not a marked mental defective. There appears to be a blunting of his moral sensibilities; instead of realizing the gravity of his position [he] regards himself a hero and appears proud of his acts. In my opinion, he is physically sound and mentally responsible for his acts.[29]

Dr. Eskridge saw no need to negotiate a Swatsonian transaction with this young murderer. As for Frank, he enjoyed seeing the doctor. "I guess he found out I'm not a lunatic," he mused.

In the end, Frank's lawyers made the curious decision not to play the insanity card. If anything, it would have slowed the process down. A "special jury" would have to try only the question of sanity. Instead, Allen hoped to build a case for mercy based on DuPre's youth and naïveté. As it happened, there was a meeting of "noted psychologists" in Atlanta. While there is no record that DuPre was actually examined by anyone other than Eskridge, Allen apparently discussed the case with two female psychoanalysts, including Dr. Elizabeth Vance of Chicago, described as an "exponent of the theory of Humanology." Humanologists believed in "analyzing people on sight" and employing the "arts" of "psychomachy, phrenology, physiognomy, pathognomy, etc." Whether from examination or from a photograph, the humanologists were consulted, and Allen announced, "This boy has a good face, an intelligent face, and he has a realization of what his thoughtlessness, his unwise associations and his inexperience have led him." They would not claim that DuPre was insane but rather that he acted while under a "nervous cataclysm." Foster agreed; it wasn't insanity, "just woeful ignorance, bad environment, and an unthinking boy impulsiveness." In mind and years, DuPre is but a child, Foster said. "There never has been a Georgia jury that would hang [white] women and children."

Frank tried to help make the case for mercy. He told reporters that if spared the noose, he'd consider himself "mighty lucky." He thought he could help other boys with a simple lesson: "Keep out of pool halls. Steer clear of booze. Give wild women a wide berth. Never carry a pistol. Beg before you steal." Boykin rolled his eyes, "Who do they think he is, 'Little

Rollo?'" he asked. The latter was the popular "very good boy" of the comics. Boykin decried such "sentimentality." He had never heard of any of these out-of-town lady doctors. To base a defense on the fact that the defendant is just a poor boy with a kind face would certainly send a dangerous message. "Criminals will go to any extent as long as they are protected by a boyish appearance," he said. Anything less than the death penalty, Boykin asserted, would be a direct blow at society.

Atlantans spent Sunday, January 22, in church. The pending trial of the Peachtree Bandit was a ready topic for sermons in the crime-rattled city. Drawing the greatest attention was the Reverend John Wesley Ham[30] in his massive Baptist Tabernacle on Luckie Street. Ham sent the papers advance word that he would "denounce maudlin sentimentality." Ham's redbrick church was topped by a flashing lighted sign that read simply, "TABERNACLE." Four thousand people could be seated in the main hall and three balconies, reminding the *Constitution*'s Woodruff of a "comfortable…modern theatre." Founded by the legendary preacher Dr. Len Broughton, the Tabernacle had been in decline. But since Ham arrived in 1918, he had brought the congregation back to its former numbers. Only thirty-nine and from Jackson, Georgia, Ham credited the resurgence to his fiery sermons, "A fire draws, a fire burns, a fire warms," he believed. That Sunday morning, Frank DuPre was put to the fire.

Ham told his flock, "This country is going to destruction morally and socially unless something is done to produce a rebirth of conscience in the matter of punishment of the law-defying murderous desperadoes who have no regard for the sacredness of human life. Life is not only cheap in the minds of the criminals, but it is cheap in the minds of the juries who deal lightly with such murderers." Do not listen, the preacher thundered, to efforts to mitigate DuPre's crime by reason of his age. "The DuPre murder has furnished the occasion for the maudlin sentimentality to come up to the front and pour out the sob stuff because he happened to be just a little under age. He possesses a criminal mind which would rank him high with the most hardened type around the age of forty. All of his prearranged plans, the execution thereof, and his actions since the day of the murder and up to the time he was caught prove that he is no youth, and has no right to be classed as such."

Ham asked his flock to contrast two scenes. First was the grieving widow and her little daughter, "who expects her daddy home that night with candy, fruit or peanuts." In the other scene was Betty Andrews, a flapper living apart from her husband. "She meets a desperado; they sit up late planning robberies. With his lynx-eyed paramour watching from across the street, her hero bandit escapes." Irby Walker was dead, Ham insisted, "because a criminal and a flapper determined upon a plan of robbery at any cost." An example must be made, Ham concluded, adding, "Anything less than capital punishment for [DuPre] would be a travesty of justice. Georgia needs to revise its conscience on capital punishment and thereby put an end to wholesale murder. The solicitors and judges are sick at heart over this miscarriage of justice. They need their arms strengthened by a healthy public sentiment and support that will reflect itself in the jury box."

Elsewhere, the Reverend William DeBardeleben of Payne Memorial Methodist Church on Hunnicutt Street chose to ask, "To what extent is society responsible?" DeBardeleben spoke of the city's unemployment crisis, saying, "We need to do more as a Christian Council to find work for these boys." He did not excuse DuPre in any way but found in his actions the signs of what ailed modern youth. The "boy bandit" was drunk; he spent too much time at "thriller" movies, in which women, diamonds and guns are the prevalent plot lines; and he went with bad women. In sum, DeBardeleben concluded that DuPre's crime was "symptomatic of our decadent home life which presages national collapse, nothing less." DeBardeleben would emerge as one of the leaders of the efforts to spare DuPre from the noose.

But Reverend Ham's words dominated the discussion. The *Constitution*'s Monday headline read, "PENALTY OF DEATH ASKED FOR DUPRE BY REV. JOHN HAM." In the Tower, DuPre told a *Journal* reporter, "I see where one of the preachers wants 'em to break my neck."

Frank's lawyers were outraged by the attention paid to Ham's tirade. Their client's chances of getting a fair trial were already slim at best. Foster condemned all three of the papers for their "wildly overdone" reports. The city was now "in a frenzy."

Chapter 7

"Some Good
Old-Fashioned Rope"

The approaching trial was discussed from pulpits, at pop stands and in printing shops. Townley & Kysor's on Alabama Street did the printing for the Southern Baptist Convention, employing "happy and satisfied non union men." They also employed women, mostly teenage girls as press feeders, a job requiring "nimble fingers to feed rapidly and accurately." J.T. Hale was shop foreman, and he'd come in Monday with the exciting news that he'd been called for the jury pool. He was soon bantering with the feeder girls, some of whom begged him to be merciful. "But he's so young, Mr. Hale!" But Hale told the girls, "I tell you this, if I get my chance, I'll stretch his neck." Back to work. The presses must be fed.

More than two thousand people were outside the Fulton County Courthouse on the cold morning of January 24, 1922. The granite nine-story monolith covered a city block, with more square footage than the state capitol. The two-story courtrooms were "lofty, well-lighted and well-ventilated." The walls, columns and coffered ceilings were done in Blue Ridge Georgia marble. Noiseless cork carpets covered the stone floors. Rows of pew-like seats would accommodate no more than two hundred observers.[31]

When the Pryor Street doors opened, there was a mad rush. To the quick went the coveted seats; there was little standing room, and many simply milled about in the halls. Judge Henry Mathews of the Macon Circuit was on the bench. A judge since 1912, the sixty-six-year-old was known as the "personification of patience." No stranger to "sensational" cases, in 1920, he oversaw the trial of four people accused in the poisoning death of the "Georgia Peach King," Fred Shepard. They were acquitted. Mathews wore a drooping gray mustache, and his shaggy eyebrows spilled over his glasses.

After Mathews was seated, there came word of a problem. Allen, DuPre's lead counsel, arrived that morning hobbling on a cane, a felt slipper on one foot. Allen's physician told the judge that Allen had two painfully infected boils. Allen apologized, but he felt he could not adequately conduct his case in such discomfort. Solicitor Boykin said he would not oppose a reasonable postponement. The judge would allow Allen forty-eight hours but stated that the trial would begin Thursday with or without the footsore attorney. The spectators left disappointed; they had come to see the Peachtree Bandit, and he had never entered the room. More, perhaps, had hoped to see the infamous Betty; she wasn't even in the building. The courtroom was cleared. The reporters could do nothing but file stories about Allen's "poisoned foot."

On Thursday morning, despite an inch of overnight snow, the crowds returned to Pryor Street. After Tuesday's aborted session, the disappointed had loitered and wandered throughout the building, disrupting county operations. The building's inner doors and gates were now locked. Mathews barked at the bailiffs to keep order. Arrest anyone who will not cooperate, he ordered. There would be no standing; anyone without a seat must leave. Those who had seats must be quiet at all times; no demonstrations would be tolerated. Coming and going would be allowed only during breaks. But still they came. "They pushed, shoved, hammered and howled to get in the courtroom all day." And those were the women. More than half the seat holders were females, mostly young and "stylishly dressed." For those kept out or unable to attend, an entrepreneurial scribbler took out an ad: "Why suffer in the crush of the Peachtree Bandit trial when I can furnish every word said during the trial for 15 cents? For 15 cents a day, I will deliver at your door a record of every word said at DuPre's trial. Drop postal quick to box H689 Constitution."

When all the seats were filled, a gavel sounded. Judge Mathews entered. Allen, still wearing a soft slipper, was at the defense table. At 9:20 a.m., Mathews said, "Let the defendant be brought into court." The prisoner had been driven from the Tower in a curtained van and placed in a holding room behind the bench. He'd been smoking and "talking trifles" with his minders. When the doorway opened, Frank DuPre emerged to be seen by many for the first time. Those who could not see stood. There was no tumult—everyone just wanted to see him. The immediate impression was how slight and young he was. "Why, he's just a boy," they whispered. Frank was cleanshaven and neatly dressed, wearing his grey suit. His hair was "polished" and combed straight back in the "Valentino fashion." Frank's father, obviously miserable, was in the first row, his head down and his clenched hands reaching out to lean on the railing behind the defense table. Frank patted his father's arm, shook hands with his lawyers and then sat between Allen and Foster. Hundreds of eyes were fixed on Frank, but the most important observers were at the press table. It would be their common observation that DuPre could not shake a curious smile. Why was he smiling? The *Journal's* O.B. Keeler decided, "There is about him an indefinable air of smug self-satisfaction."

The DuPre team had decided against seeking a change of venue or making an insanity plea. Instead, they entered a plea of not guilty to the charge of murder. Allen would claim that what occurred at Kaiser's was not murder but what the state of Georgia defined as voluntary manslaughter. In Georgia, circa 1922, if A was accused of killing B, A could claim that he was being assaulted by B and that, fearing serious personal injury or death at the hands of B, acted under the excitement of passion to protect himself against B. "The killing must be the result of that sudden, violent impulse of passion supposed to be irresistible."[32] That was the crime of voluntary manslaughter.

Allen's argument, bluntly put, was that "even a criminal has the right to self-defense." It was plainly a long shot. Beyond that, all that remained was an abject plea for mercy. Foster told reporters, "[DuPre] is young and woefully ignorant and used his pistol on a wild impulse, caused by whiskey and fright. We expect to show that he was prompted by older heads who balked at the risk they urged DuPre to take." The jury, he hoped, would spare this boy's life and instead put him in a Georgia prison for the rest of his life.

Selecting the jury took most of the morning. Eighty-four potential jurors had been called. By statute, at least, they were expected to be "experienced, upright and intelligent." In Georgia, all potential jurymen were asked three questions: (1) Have you formed an opinion on this case? (2) Do you have any bias either for or against the prisoner? (3) Is your mind perfectly impartial between the State and the accused? However, with this being a death penalty case, there was a fourth question: Are you conscientiously opposed to capital punishment? Any man who answered yes to that final question was to be excused. Allen sought to add a fifth question: "Have you heard or read the sermon delivered by the Rev. Ham on January 22?" Allen called the sermon "highly inflammatory and prejudicial," and he would strike any juryman who answered affirmatively. Boykin objected. Mathews allowed Allen to ask a more general question: "Have you been influenced by any sermon bearing on this case?" The process went slowly; twenty out of the sixty-three men called said they would never vote to hang a man. They were dismissed. As for Allen's fifth question, no one admitted that he had heard or read the Ham sermon. Among the jurors selected was J. Tifton Hale, pressman at Townley & Kysor.

The jury was seated in two rows of six to the right of the bench. Boykin read his list of twenty-five witnesses. Betty Andrews's name was not on it. The trial began with a bailiff's call for Mrs. Irby Walker. The widow of the slain Pinkerton operative entered dressed in mourning black. The trail of her skirt may have even brushed DuPre's leg as she passed the defense table. Frank did not lift his eyes from the table. Gladys Walker was composed though her eyes were reddened with recent tears. She displayed "clean cut, pretty features." The *Constitution* called her appearance "the most dramatic incident" of the day. In fact, the prosecution's questions were routine, asking how long she had been married, the age of her daughter, etc. Her husband, she stated, had been her sole support. "And now?" Boykin asked. She replied, "He is dead and lies buried in Alabama." The police had returned to her the bloody suit her husband had been wearing. She could not bear to look at it. She identified the hat her husband had worn. Holding the hat so that the jury could see where a bullet had ripped through it, Boykin asked the witness, "Was there a bullet hole in this hat when your husband left your home that morning?" Softly, she answered, "No, there was not." Allen had only a single question for the widow Walker: "How much did your husband weigh?" She put his weight at 132 pounds.

The next four witnesses were Kaiser's employees. The manager, Nat Ullman, recalled that he was in his office dealing with the mail when Mrs. Phillips asked him to wait on a curious customer. He thought to have a whisper with detective Walker, who discreetly "took the door." Ullman said the defendant seemed uneasy and would not look him in the eye. He refused to see a ring priced at $500, insisting on the diamond ring in the window. Ullman retrieved the desired ring, which the young man took in his left hand between his finger and thumb as if to more closely inspect the stone. The man then turned and ran for the door. Walker blocked his path, but at first, according to Ullman, he merely put his hand firmly on DuPre's shoulder. DuPre refused to stop, and there was a struggle. The two men stumbled back into the store. Ullman then heard two shots fired, and Walker dropped to the floor. He identified the defendant, Frank DuPre, as the man who entered Kaiser's on that afternoon.

Allen gingerly rose to question the witness. Using enlarged photographs of the jewelry showroom, Allen went over with Ullman the exact positioning of everyone that afternoon. Most especially, he "minutely" quizzed the witness as to the movements of the slain detective. Allen wanted the jury to consider whether Irby Walker might have used excessive force. There is a "merchant's privilege" that allows a merchant or his agent (i.e., a security guard) to detain a suspected thief. "Reasonable force" may be used. But what if DuPre did not know that Walker was a store detective? What if he feared that he was simply being jumped by a stranger, who might well have been armed? Might he then have fought to save his own life, making this voluntary manslaughter? Ullman admitted Walker was not in any kind of uniform. He was in plainclothes, a suit and topcoat, not unlike what DuPre was wearing. He showed no badge, nor did Walker ever identify himself as a lawman. Walker had a gun. But Ullman insisted there was no excessive force; Walker simply blocked DuPre's exit, and a struggle ensued.

The other three Kaiser's workers were called, each giving only slightly variant descriptions of the horrible scene they had witnessed. Mrs. Phillips recalled that the man had said he needed a ring because he was about to get married. An ever-watchful reporter noted that Frank "flashed a broad smile" at this. Donald Drukenmiller said the defendant had seemed "perfectly sober." After the shooting, Drukenmiller chased the bandit into the Kimball House. He believed that the bullet that struck Comptroller West "may very well have been meant for me." Finally, Paul Bonebrake gave the most detailed description of the deadly struggle. After the gunshots, he heard Walker cry out, "Somebody better get me a doctor." Bonebrake added, "He died in my arms." Allen pressed Bonebrake about the shots. Was he certain he heard two? How rapidly in succession? Might there have been three? Did Walker pull his gun? Did he fire his gun? Boykin objected to the questions as immaterial. Allen, sore foot and all, "whirled" upon the solicitor. "I am running this side of the case," he shouted.

Just seven weeks after being shot in the face, a frail-looking Graham West entered the witness box. West was a lanky, good-looking man but bore an "ugly" scar along his chin and jaw. Allen objected that West had no business being a witness in this case. DuPre was on trial for slaying Irby Walker; the shooting of West was a separate action, and West knew nothing about what happened at Kaiser's. Boykin reminded the judge that in a death penalty case, the State must show malice. DuPre had fired wildly on bystanders, striking Mr. West with one of those shots, dramatic proof that the accused had acted with an "abandoned and malignant heart." Mathews allowed West to be sworn in.

The comptroller, despite his appearance, spoke in a strong, clear voice. He had lunched at the Kimball House with a friend, and they were then walking through the revolving doors from the hotel into the passageway leading to Peachtree. The defendant burst through that street door and stumbled toward them, his right hand plunged deep into his overcoat pocket. The young man rushed past them and then fell. West recalled seeing ahead of him the excitement out on Peachtree. In seconds, some men came in that door with shouts of, "There he is!" West said he turned to look behind him and took perhaps a step toward the man, who was still on the ground. The man pulled a gun from his overcoat and fired one shot. "I felt a stinging sensation in the side of my face, and I fell to the ground," he said. West passed out, and he remembered nothing until he woke to the sound of voices saying his name. Throughout West's testimony, DuPre sat with downcast eyes.

The stolen ring, identified by Ullman, was in Boykin's hands when he began to question Max Silverman. The aged Chattanooga pawnbroker's English was very poor. Silverman recognized the ring as the one that was brought to his shop by a young man. "Is that man here today?" asked Boykin. Silverman nodded. Boykin asked that he point him out. Silverman's finger found Frank DuPre. Boykin gave up the witness. Allen's cross-examination was hampered by the witness's inability or refusal to understand the questions. Yes, Silverman admitted, his nephew Max Abelson ran a loan shop in Atlanta. "Isn't it a fact that DuPre came to you because he had been sent by Mr. Abelson?" "No, no, no," the old man replied. Silverman would not admit that he knew the ring was stolen. "Weren't you in the least suspicious that this young man—'John Doe'—would be in possession of such a valuable ring?" The pawnbroker shrugged—he thought the lad had an honest face. If that were true, Allen pressed, and this was an honest transaction, then Silverman should have been willing to offer much more for such a valuable ring. Silverman noted that the two men had haggled over the price, something common in most pawnshop deals. Silverman insisted that as soon as he learned the ring was stolen, he told the police. But Allen asked if it were true that a Chattanooga detective came in to the shop while DuPre was there and yet Silverman said nothing. Police were always coming in, he replied. Mathews finally interrupted this colloquy: "Mr. Allen, these things that happened in Chattanooga—are they material to what happened in Atlanta?" "Perhaps not, your honor," he replied, adding that he was attacking the credibility of an important prosecution witness. Mathews frowned and said, "Well, Mr. Silverman is not on trial here. Move on."

More witnesses followed to describe DuPre's flight up Peachtree and through the Kimball House: terrified shoppers, hotel workers and even a pool player. Frederick Shalloway ran the haberdashery off the hotel lobby. He testified that DuPre came in around 1:30 p.m. and idly looked at ties. He bought one (for ninety-five cents), took off the tie he'd been wearing and replaced it with the new one. The customer then went out the Pryor Street door, turning toward Wall Street.

That ended the first day. DuPre was removed to a private elevator that took him down to a van. The commotion at the courthouse exit was intense, and several people in the crowd were knocked down. The *Journal's* Keeler cracked that either the city's unemployment is as bad as folks say it is or that "Atlanta has an ample leisure class." Elsewhere, the newsstands were soon sold out; the *Georgian* put out six editions that day. It was plain that Frank's smirking attitude had not gone unnoticed. Friday morning's *Constitution* headlined, "DUPRE, SMILING, HEARS WITNESSES TELL OF KILLING."

More sleet and ice fell through the night, but there were no empty seats Friday morning. Frank wore the same suit, his hair neatly combed; one reporter thought he was "dressed as for an outing" in "tea hound" style. Boykin opened day two by reading into the record the now-famous "boneheads" letter. Again, Frank was seen to "laugh quietly." The solicitor then called Detective Sturdivant. Over Allen's objections, the detective told the jury about DuPre's movements from the day of the shooting to his arrest in Detroit. Sturdivant read DuPre's confession. Allen's cross-examination was laden with sarcasm. "DuPre just started confessing? Of course, you didn't threaten him in anyway?" Sturdivant denied any threats. Had DuPre been told that a confession might help him avoid the gallows? "No, sir," Sturdivant answered. Allen returned to his seat.

Clifford Buckley, the taxi driver, was the last witness for the state. He described meeting Jack Worth, who introduced him to DuPre that afternoon. The defendant said he needed to get to Chattanooga. Buckley wanted $100, but they settled on $90. He admitted accompanying DuPre to the pawnshop but swore that he took no role in the negotiations. Once DuPre paid the fare, Buckley said he left the bandit at Chattanooga station and never saw him again. Allen got Buckley to admit that he knew his passenger was the Peachtree Bandit and that he agreed to help a killer escape to get money for Christmas presents. Buckley conceded that he was now out of a job and facing prosecution.

The DuPre defense team would call no witnesses. By doing so, it retained the significant privilege of speaking last to the jury. But whom could it have called? An "alienist?" They had chosen not to make an insanity plea. Character witnesses? Unhelpful. Instead, the plan was to go all in on the "unsworn statement" of Frank DuPre. Under Georgia law, derived from the historic "common law," a criminal defendant could not be sworn to testify to the truth, the whole truth. The traditional presumption was that the accused would automatically lie. Instead, the Georgia code read, "In all criminal trials in this State, the prisoner shall have the right to make to the court and jury such statement in the case as he or she may deem proper in his or her defense, said statement is not to be under oath, and to have such force only as the jury may think right to give it."[33]

Frank would be allowed to speak to the jury for as long as he liked. The prosecution could not cross-examine him, but at the same time, his lawyers were restricted from questioning him, helping him, prompting him, leading him on or stopping him short. The Georgia Supreme Court had held that "counsel for the accused cannot ask the accused questions or make suggestions to him when he is making his statement to the court and jury." Thus, this final appeal to the jury was left in the hands and words of an eighteen-year-old. In 1874, a Michigan court had foreseen the problems with this, nothing that "if [the defendant] is unlearned, unaccustomed to speak in public assemblies, or to put together his thoughts in consecutive order anywhere, it will not be surprising if his explanation is incoherent, or if it overlooks important circumstances." It wasn't until 1961 that the U.S. Supreme Court, in *Ferguson v. Georgia*, struck Georgia's "unsworn statement" provision, by then the only remaining such practice in the nation. And not so much because these unsworn statements hurt the prosecution but rather because so many defendants botched their opportunity so badly while their attorneys could do nothing but look on in horror.[34]

This was Frank's only chance. Allen and his colleagues really had only one week to prepare. We have to presume that as experienced defenders, they made it clear that this statement was his only opportunity to impress the jury that he was deserving of mercy. He needed to express his regret for what had happened. At the very least, he had to simply say, "I'm sorry." It wouldn't bring Irby Walker back to life, but it might save his own.

As Frank left the defense table to approach the witness stand, many spectators stood as glowering deputies waved them back down. Frank walked steadily, almost quickly; the *Journal* detected once again a "faint smile." The *Constitution* thought, "He seemed not a bit embarrassed and spoke in a voice of depth, strength, and with considerable more command of English than his story of limited advantages as to schooling would have indicated." He used no notes. The *Georgian* reported, "He eyed the jury squarely, losing the shifty gaze attributed to him. He spoke clearly and was understood by all." It was high noon. He spoke for less than fifteen minutes, occasionally losing his train of thought. He paused frequently to brush his hair back. At one point, he asked Allen if he was saying too much. Allen told him to simply say what he wanted to. "But I don't want to annoy the jury," Frank worried. Following is the verbatim account as it appeared in the next day's *Constitution*:

My father is a blacksmith, and I was born on August 16, 1903. We lived at Americus and Cedartown and then in Atlanta. I went to the Davis Street School and the Baptist Tabernacle. I understand that the Reverend Ham is pastor of that church now. My father worked at the Charleston Navy Yard, and I did too when we moved there from Atlanta. I worked there until my mother died. We came back to Atlanta. Then my father and I toured Montgomery, Mobile, New Orleans and Birmingham looking for work. My father finally went back to the Charleston Navy Yard, and I went to work in a garage. I worked there for a while and then got a job as a file clerk in the signal corps of the Southeastern Army headquarters. I stayed there five months and then my father went to work for the Seaboard Air Line. I got a job with the Scenic Film Company and then got laid off. I enlisted in the Navy and stayed in a while but finally got a special discharge. I went back to the Scenic Film Company, but hard times came along and I got laid off again because they didn't need so many employees. I went around looking for work. I was half starved most of the time and didn't have anything much to wear. I couldn't get a job. Then one night, I met Mr. Reville, and he was staying at the Aragon Hotel. He asked me to go up there with him, and I did. In his room, he showed me $140 in money. I got that money, and in the morning, I went away with it before he got up. This money kept me up until I did the Davis-Freeman job. After I got those rings, I met a bootlegger, and he told me that Jack Worth would handle them for me. I met Worth in a poolroom by appointment and asked him for $150 for the smaller ring. He finally gave me $125, getting the money from a savings bank. I told Worth I wanted $500 for the larger ring, but he didn't have that much money. Then I met Max Abelson, and he gave me $300 for the larger ring. After this I went to Charleston for a few days and when I got back I met Jack Worth, and he suggested that I cut the show glass of the Sanford jewelry store (64 Peachtree) and take out a whole tray of rings. I was afraid to do this and wouldn't attempt it. Now, about this Kaiser Jewelry robbery. I want to say first that Betty Andrews didn't know anything about it beforehand. She did not persuade me to do it. I was drunk at the time or I probably wouldn't have done it. I bought a half pint of whiskey from a man named Hawkeye on Marietta Street and drank every bit of it. If Betty had seen me in the condition I was in before I stole the ring, she would have locked me in the room, I know. When I turned to run out of the Kaiser store, Walker grabbed me. That's the last thing I remember. I believe Walker would have killed me if I didn't fire that shot. When Walker grabbed me, the first thing I remember I was in a haberdashery store on Pryor Street buying a necktie. I called the Spider Taxicab Company but couldn't make them understand where I wanted the taxi to come. So I hung up the receiver and took off my overcoat. I then walked across Pryor Street to the other side and then on Pryor as far as Auburn Avenue. Then I crossed through Auburn to Peachtree and on to Forsyth and back to the Childs Hotel, where I changed my clothes. I went to Betty's room and told her I was in trouble. I gave her $8, telling her to go to the Cecil Hotel and register as Mrs. DuPre. After that I went to the Lily White restaurant to eat. Later, I went to the Strand Theatre (Peachtree) when I found Worth. I told him that I did the Kaiser job, and he remarked that I certainly had guts. We met Max Abelson, and Worth asked him to buy the ring. Abelson wouldn't do it, but he told Worth that a pawnbroker named Silverman in Chattanooga would. After that I went to the Strand Theatre, and when I came out I met Worth again. He introduced me to Buckley, and told Buckley that I had done the Kaiser job. We agreed for Buckley to take me to Chattanooga for $90. I asked Worth for some money to check out of the Childs Hotel, and he gave me $9. I met Betty at 5:45 in front of the YMCA. While I was talking to her, Buckley drove up. I told Betty to go back to the Cecil and pickup and go with me to Chattanooga. She went on away. She stayed so long that I telephoned her. Then she said she couldn't find her sister and for me to go on ahead and then send her money to come on later. We went away without her. At Chattanooga, we stored the car and looked for Silverman's pawnshop that Abelson told us about. We found it. An old man was alone there. He was "old man Silverman." I showed him the ring and told him Abelson had sent me. While we were there, a detective came in, but the old man said not to worry and that he was a friend of the detective. He said that he couldn't buy the ring until he talked to his son. We went out and went to a restaurant and ate something. Silverman had said he would give me $700 for the ring. When we met young Abe Silverman, he only had $326. He gave me that and told. me when I needed more to write and let him know. I told Abe Silverman *to go with Buckley to the car and get my suitcase, which he did. He met me at the train on which I went to Norfolk. In Norfolk, I registered at the Monticello Hotel under the name of F.B. Parker. I wired Buckley $40 to give Betty. I went to the Western Union office at 5:00 that afternoon and asked if there was a telegram there for Frank DuPre. A girl clerk tipped me off that two detectives were there waiting for me. I stayed in Norfolk until December 21st, when I read that Atlanta detectives were watching Betty's mail. Then I went to Detroit, arriving there December 23rd. I searched for work a long time but finally had to write back to Silverman in Chattanooga for the rest of the money promised on the ring. When I went to the post office to get his reply, of course, I was picked up by the Detroit detectives.*

Having spoken for fifteen minutes and worried that he was rambling, Frank stopped. The halt became awkward. From the defense table, Allen could do nothing but ask, "Is that all, Frank?" The lawyer would never have been allowed to ask, "And you're sorry, aren't you, Frank?" Boykin would have erupted. Frank nodded that he was done. Mathews said he could return to his seat. Frank walked slowly back to the table, briefly embracing his sobbing father.

That had not gone well. All Frank had done was re-confess as if he enjoyed sharing the saga of the Peachtree Bandit with a new audience. Asking to be excused on grounds of being drunk was a nonstarter. Drunkenness was no defense. He specifically exonerated Betty, putting paid to any chance to portray him as a boy led on by a wicked woman. Telling the jury that he thought Walker might kill him was helpful for the voluntary manslaughter argument, but he weakened the point by then claiming that he was too drunk to remember what had happened that afternoon. The description of his flight and the efforts to hock the ring undercut the case that he was a poor, naïve boy. Ultimately, the greatest flaw was the absence of a single word of regret to Mrs. Walker or Comptroller West, both of whom were seated in the courtroom. Instead of remorse, he remembered with pride how Worth told him he had "guts." Frank had once told reporters that if spared, he would help other boys. He so desperately needed to make that same pledge to this jury, but he sat down with the words unsaid. He failed to give the jury a single reason for consideration. It was a completely missed opportunity. Like hundreds of defendants before and after him, he was "set adrift in an uncharted sea with nothing to guide him, with the result that his statement in most cases either does him no good or is positively hurtful."

Judge Mathews gave each side two hours for their closing summary. As the defense had presented no evidence (DuPre's statement was not considered evidence), they held the important right to open and close the final arguments.

Heyward and Foster, in turn, spoke first. Heyward's target was Betty Andrews. DuPre was a motherless lad desperate for female support and attention. He had the misfortune to meet Betty Andrews, and he became infatuated. He was no stronger than Adam, David or Samson, all of whom lost favor with God for a woman. Heyward quoted Proverbs 5:17: "The lips of a forbidden woman drip honey, and her speech is smoother than oil, but in the end she is bitter as wormwood, sharp as a two-edged sword." Biblical references were always useful.

Foster attacked the absent Jack Worth, the "real villain" of this tragedy. A "craven and a coward, [Worth] didn't have the nerve to commit these robberies, but he did have the cunning to put this boy up to them," he said. Yet the boy alone faces the noose. "Will not the ends of justice be served by his confinement for life…to reflect on his crime? Isn't that the real punishment?"

Boykin was assisted by his deputy, Ed Stephens. One prominent Atlanta attorney, Rube Arnold, had called them a "pair of bloodthirsty headhunters."[35] Stephens scoffed at the notion that DuPre was owed consideration for his age. "This is no kindergarten boy," he stated. "This is a ruthless killer who spiked his courage with bootleg liquor." According to Stephens, DuPre had taken "the crimson life blood from another man to buy silken baubles for a woman who is herself crimson with crime." Atlanta residents were demanding action to stem this wave of violent crime. Stephens said that there were laws on the books for a reason. "Gentlemen, if you don't hang this man who deliberately planned a crime and then shot Irby Walker in cold blood, then you ought to go forth to dig up all the others who have been hanged and apologize to them."

Boykin said they had heard much about repentance, yet DuPre sat in court "smirking and smiling." There was no repentance but rather more threats in that "boneheads" letter. DuPre had even joked that he was sure that Mr. Graham West would now "mind his own business." As for any thought that the jurymen might have to spare DuPre on behalf of his grieving father, Boykin reminded them "of little Alda Walker, who grieves too for her slain father." Echoing the words of Reverend Ham's sermon, Boykin ended with the following: "We need more men, more rugged men, with the courage and manhood to put the rope around the neck of desperadoes like this. What we need in Atlanta is a rebirth of the hanging law. We need some good old-fashioned rope."

Allen spoke last, employing his "impressive and sonorous voice." Allen had listened to Boykin condemn DuPre for calling the city detectives "boneheads." Allen threw up his hands and said, "My goodness alive, John has called them a whole lot worse things than that." Laughter broke the tension, but only briefly. Unsmiling, Allen walked to the state's table where the two past mortal enemies, Boykin and Detective Poole, were seated. "Look at them now," he said, "united to hang this boy."

Allen sought to make a case for voluntary manslaughter. DuPre did not intend to kill Irby Walker, he argued. When DuPre bolted for the door, a man he did not know and who was dressed in plainclothes grabbed him roughly. DuPre told the Detroit police he thought Walker was going for his gun. A store guard does not have unlimited powers. "What was the most natural thought that would pop into this inexperienced boy's mind? That Walker was going to beat the life out him." Even a fugitive from justice has the right to defend himself from an attack he fears may be fatal. In his statement, Frank told the jurymen he had feared for his life. Allen asserted, "If Frank shot under that belief, then he is not guilty of murder."

Allen closed with an appeal for mercy. Boykin's talk of rope "was an insult to an intelligent jury." DuPre's life should be spared not out of "maudlin sentimentality" but rather as an act of simple justice. Where was Jack Worth? Where was the pawnbroker? Silverman was claiming his share of the reward money. Allen sneered that "the old Shylock would seek his pound of flesh." Yet this naïve boy must go to the gallows? "Look at him," Allen told the jury. "He is either crazy as a bat or an inexperienced crook. Either way, he doesn't deserve to hang. If you take the life of this eighteen-and-a-half-year-old boy, you would be committing a travesty of justice." Allen's words brought out more than a few handkerchiefs. Eyes were dried, noses blown.

But Georgia law in 1922 was clear: "the punishment for persons convicted of murder shall be death." There were two exceptions. If the judge thought the conviction was based solely on circumstantial evidence, he had the discretion to commute the sentence to life in prison. More relevant to this case, however, is the fact that a jury had the absolute right to return a verdict of guilty with a recommendation for mercy. The convicted would then be "confined in the penitentiary for the rest of his life." The jury's decision was irreversible—no judge could intervene.[36]

In his charge to the jury, Mathews defined murder and voluntary manslaughter: "I charge you to find that if Walker was killed because of DuPre's desire to escape with a stolen diamond, it is murder." But if it appeared that Walker had used a "disproportionate amount of force," arousing in DuPre "an ungovernable passion leading him to believe his person was in danger," they might consider a verdict of voluntary manslaughter. Mathews reminded the twelve men that if they found DuPre guilty of murder and they wished to extend mercy, they must "indicate that fact in your verdict." But the judge did not stop there, adding, "You are citizens of this county…you heard the evidence, the jury is supposed to know what ought to be done with reference to fixing the punishment. The court has no suggestion to make to you with reference to that; you may consider what the object of punishment is, consider all the facts and circumstances of the case, circumstances of mitigation or palliation, or circumstances of aggravation, anything that you think ought to be considered as bearing upon the question of what punishment you shall fix."

The jury was let out at 6:30 on a winter Friday evening. Frank smoked "innumerable cigarettes." The lawyers waited around, sparring with the reporters. Allen was confident that the jury would be merciful. Boykin was disgusted by the "loafers" who had jammed the courthouse for two days to see the Peachtree Bandit. "Is it any wonder, then, that this sort of stuff goes to the head of a man like DuPre?" he asked. At 10:00 p.m., the jury reported exhaustion and asked to return in the morning. DuPre returned to the Tower. Bailiffs herded the disappointed crowds out of a darkened courthouse.

A "characteristically eager throng" was back at 8:00 a.m. on Saturday. Mrs. Walker and her daughter arrived at 9:00 a.m. The widow had been in court throughout, following everything with "deep and absorbing interest." Word of a verdict came at 10:20 a.m. The lawyers resumed their places. Frank was brought in. He looked pale but walked steadily. For several minutes, he sat apparently unperturbed. Judge Mathews took the bench and warned against any demonstrations. At 10:45, the jury entered. Their grim faces were thought to be a "bad augury" for the accused. The foreman was Henry Fridell, an Inman Park paperhanger. Mathews asked Fridell if the jury had reached its verdict. Fridell answered that it had. "We find the defendant guilty." Every ear in the room strained to hear any additional words, any petition for mercy or life imprisonment. Fridell said no more. He stood silent. That was that. No more than a loud murmur swept the room. DuPre gave what seemed to be a knowing smile, as if to say he was not surprised. The *Journal* thought the smile "was near to being a laugh." The *Georgian* agreed that DuPre's "composure bore a tinge of recklessness." DuPre's father, seated behind him, sobbed. The *Constitution* saw DuPre turn with a "half sneering smile" to pat his father's arm.

Allen announced that he would seek a new trial; Mathews set a hearing for February 18. There was complete silence as Mathews spoke the required words: "Let the defendant stand up. It is the order of the court that you be hanged by the neck until you are dead on the 10th day of March 1922 by the sheriff of Fulton County in the common jail between the hours of 10am and 3pm, and may God have mercy on your soul." Frank showed no discernible emotion. The deputies shackled his wrists and led him out. Reporters surrounded Fridell, who said there had been twelve ballots. There were two holdouts Friday night. Before they left for their hotel, Fridell said they prayed. "We needed some divine guidance," he said. The last holdouts were swayed, and the jury had reached a unanimous verdict by 10:00 a.m. Mrs. Walker had also prayed, telling reporters, "My prayers have been answered." When tracked down by the *Georgian*, Jack Worth refused to comment.

At the Tower, Betty Andrews wailed. She vowed to save Frank from the noose. "When I get out, I will devote all to saving Frank," she said. "He is a good boy. We will go to the Governor, I shall not rest." If all failed, she promised to stand by his side at the gallows. Betty denounced Mrs. Walker, whose daily presence she thought had influenced the jury against Frank. "I hear she laughed. She must have a heart of stone." The bandit's father was inconsolable. "I can't talk now," he said. "I will fight for my boy."

Meanwhile, his boy, Frank DuPre, was back at the Tower in time for Saturday lunch. He ate heartily and asked for more pie.

Chapter 8

"Somebody Loves
This Poor Devil"

At the Tower, Frank was moved to "Cell No. 5, North Wing." Nearby was "Old John" Williams, awaiting his move to the state prison farm for causing the deaths of eleven Negroes who'd been held in peonage in Jasper County.[37] A white man, Williams had arranged with the local sheriffs to bring him their "troublemakers." He quite literally worked them to death on his two-thousand-acre plantation. Williams told a reporter that he was stunned to see the young and slight DuPre. "It's a shame, you know," he offered.

Sheriff James Lowry was the man tasked to do the hanging. He had hanged several men since taking office in 1917, most recently a rapist in 1920.[38] But Lowry had never hanged a white man. The last white man hanged in Fulton was wife-killer Robert Clay in 1912. From the day he was arrested, Clay refused to speak until, days before he was hanged, he complained that the Tower coffee wasn't hot enough. Sheriff Lowry promised that, white or black, the gallows would be ready for Frank DuPre when needed.

Henry Allen told the *Constitution*, "Only now does DuPre understand the horrible situation he is in. Maybe now we can try to get him to help us." Some prominent help was nearby. In Spartanburg, South Carolina, the former big-league ballplayer turned evangelist Billy Sunday[39] was holding one of his celebrated revivals. He preached three times daily, mixing "scripture and modern slang with a rapidity that leaves his audience almost dizzy." Sunday had followed the DuPre trial in the papers. On February 1, he wrote to Governor Hardwick, "I hope you will exercise that clemency typical of the big heart and generosity of the South." According to his biographer, Robert

Martin, Sunday held no strong views regarding hanging but had a "soft and sympathetic side" and an ear for injustice.[40] Hardwick assured Sunday that any appeal would get his "careful and conscientious attention."

Hardwick's office released both letters to the Atlanta papers. From the Tower, Frank sent Sunday a letter of thanks:

> *Mr. Sunday, I want to tell you how much I appreciate your kindness. I have been reading your sermons that you preached in Spartanburg, and I think they are wonderful. I want to tell you that I think you are a gift to the human race and you should be appreciated by everybody for your great work. Mr. Sunday, would you please say a prayer for me? I certainly will appreciate it if you will. I end my letter with many thanks to you. Yours devotedly, Frank B. DuPre.*

Sunday read Frank's letter aloud to friends, and his "voice shook" when he got to the requested prayer. The prayer was duly offered, but Sunday played no further role in the clemency battle.

Another clergyman climbed his Atlanta pulpit on the Sunday following the verdict. At the Central Baptist Church on Cooper Street, Reverend Caleb Ridley told his congregation that it was a "great mistake" to rush DuPre to trial in a city inflamed by "preachers, silly women, and asinine men [who] rushed into the newspapers and condemned him before the courts got a whack at him." He denounced the Tabernacle's Reverend Ham, stating, "It is no province of a preacher to damn a man and demand his death." In tears, Ridley asked for prayers for the young man languishing in a death cell. "Somebody loves this poor devil," he added. In addition to his pastoral duties at Central Baptist, the Reverend Ridley was the Imperial Kludd—more commonly called the chaplain—of the Georgia Ku Klux Klan. Georgia did not hang white folk. Ridley wrote to Governor Hardwick requesting a meeting on some future date. For the present, however, he was "out of the city so much, Ku Kluxin' around."[41]

Two weeks later, with Frank's father in the pews, Ridley demanded a new trial. Frank was a motherless boy who led a life as "straight as a string" until he fell in with a bad crowd. What chance was there for a fair trial in a city inflamed by a rabid crime-obsessed press? "If we have to make an example of someone, for God's sake do not begin on this child," he pleaded.

Days later, Ridley had what was called a "serious nervous breakdown." For a decade, he had used his pulpit to rail against race-mixers. A leader on the Dixie Defense Committee, he denounced all things Jewish, Catholic and, of course, Negro. Many fellow clergymen, Baptist and otherwise, thought his Klan role had become intolerable. Ridley buckled under the strain. He took an extended vacation and did not return until April. In his first sermon back, with typical rhetoric, Ridley announced he would continue to work to save the bandit's neck. "It's an outrage to take his life when that old rascal in Jasper County [Old John Williams], who killed a whole field full of niggers, is sitting tonight, smoking his pipe in peace," he said.[42]

Meanwhile, the Tabernacle's Reverend Ham ignored his critics, declaring himself quite satisfied with the verdict. An editorial in one Columbus newspaper called him a "disgusting...sensational pulpiteer" and added that if the Atlanta papers just ignored him, few would notice. But Ham was unrepentant and announced a new six-week series of Sunday evening sermons: certain movies as factories of crime; certain cheap hotels as factories of crime; the pools rooms as factories of crime; the dance halls as factories of immorality; the movies as factories of immorality and free love; and the taxicab, the tiger and the flapper.

The Fulton County Grand Jury quickly indicted Worth, Buckley, Wiley, Geoghan and Betty Andrews as accessories after the fact of murder. Once depicted as a great "gang of jewel thieves," they all got off rather lightly. Worth was tried first before Judge John Humphries. The rumor was that Frank DuPre would be the star witness, but Worth's attorney, Len Guillebeau, vowed to block the bandit from testifying under the Napoleonic Code tradition, which held that a condemned man is considered legally dead. The dead don't speak. Solicitor Boykin's team opted to rely on Buckley, the driver, who testified that Worth came to him that Thursday afternoon with DuPre. Worth introduced Frank as "the man who killed the detective."

Max Abelson, the Atlanta "jeweler," swore that Worth came to his shop that Thursday asking to hock a "large stone, cheap." Abelson, of course, insisted that he had no idea the stone was the one from the Kaiser's job. He had done nothing unlawful.

A jury found Worth guilty of "harboring and assisting Frank DuPre to escape." Humphries gave Worth the maximum three years in prison (later reduced to one). Worth "evidenced great anguish" at the sentence; in the seats, Mrs. Worth, holding her baby, "little Jack Jr.," went into a swoon. It was a "touching scene."

At Buckley's trial, the jobless cabbie pleaded guilty. His lawyer told Humphries, "He is a mere boy, your honor, who thought he was doing the right thing by helping another in distress." The "mere boy" appeal seemed to work in the case of twenty-five-year-old Buckley, who got a year on the prison farm.

Vincent Geoghan pleaded guilty to a minor charge and was fined $150. George Wiley was never prosecuted for anything.

Betty Andrews's day in court came on March 4. Soberly dressed in a brown suit, Betty wore her hair in the "current Mary Pickford fashion." The actress would have been proud. Betty "fainted" three times, once in the waiting room. Her attorney, Fred Harrison, and a matron helped her into court. Boykin had once boasted that a "mountain of evidence" implicated Betty in the planning of the Kaiser's robbery. Thus it was a surprise when the solicitor announced that all charges were being dropped. Boykin told Humphries that Betty had not known DuPre's plan in advance. At worst, she had briefly "harbored" him after the shooting. However, in consideration for her assistance in the efforts to apprehend the bandit, that charge would be "noll prossed."

Instead, Boykin said Betty would plead guilty to a "statutory offense," a legal euphemism often used for sex crimes such as contributing to the delinquency of a minor. When asked how she pleaded, Betty shrieked, "I will never plead guilty to anything!" Harrison got her under control, begging Humphries to understand that his client was "poorly developed mentally." She had spent four years in the first grade in Gainesville, and her teachers recalled that she had a "positively dull mind." Humphries responded, "Then Atlanta is surely no place for a girl like her." He would suspend her year's sentence at the women's farm at Milledgeville and place her in the custody of her father. Betty was, in effect, exiled to Hall County.

———•—

Frank DuPre's hanging date of March 10, 1922, came and went. His appeal did not come up until mid-March. The train from Atlanta that arrived at Macon's Terminal Station was crowded for a Saturday morning. The lawyers for the two sides, a few witnesses, reporters and quondam "interested parties" made the journey. A crowd waited on the steps of the Bibb County Courthouse. To the disappointment of the Maconite curious, the bandit remained in Atlanta. The locals were rewarded with a glimpse of Mrs. Irby Walker and the small figure of the bandit's father.

The hearing before Judge Mathews lasted eight hours. Allen made two claims. Firstly, he asserted that Mathews had not properly instructed the trial jury on sentencing. That argument will be explored in greater detail below in the case of *DuPre v. Georgia*.

The great bulk of the long day was dedicated to the second point, in which Allen asserted that five members of the jury were prejudiced against his client. One, as we have seen, was J.T. Hale, the print-shop foreman. Two young press feeders had sworn in an affidavit that Hale talked of the chance to "stretch" DuPre's neck. Allen had similar affidavits accusing four others of making like remarks. Ira Moultrie allegedly vowed, "If I was on the jury, I'd break his neck." Juror William Howell was heard to say, "If I'm caught on the DuPre case, I'll hang him if I have anything to do with it." James Brannon supposedly said, "There's no doubt that DuPre ought to hang." Lastly, George Harris was overheard telling a friend that "DuPre ought to get his neck broke."

Boykin's investigators had also been at work and claimed that those who impugned the jurors had biases of their own. Howell's accuser, for example, had a long-standing personal feud with the juryman. As for Hale, the printer swore that he was just "kidding around" with some shop girls. Boykin said he considered prosecuting the girls—Emma Coleman and Frances McNeal—for a flagrant case of contempt of court. It was a bitter battle of affidavits. At one point, Allen erupted, "Your Honor, they have the testimony of a few dagos and we have the East Point Chief of Police!" But Boykin's key witness was Fridell, the jury foreman who swore that none of the impugned jurors had shown any prejudice. In fact, he recalled that Brannon was the last holdout for the death sentence.

Boykin said Allen's appeal amounted to nothing but a few "flyspecked technicalities." Referring to those "sentimental schoolgirls" and "maudlin sentimentalists" behind the appeal, he wondered, "Do they ever think about this widow in court?" Pointing to the press table, Boykin said there has been too much "slush" written about the "boy" bandit and too many pictures of Betty Andrews with "her lipstick and curly locks." None of that should influence the court. "If ever a case deserved hanging, this was it."

Allen spoke for ninety minutes. Since when, he asked Mathews, was the purity of a jury trial a "fly-specked technicality?" His client had been swept to a trial while the prosecutors, the newspapers and even the preachers cried out to hang him. "Your honor knows what a mob was at that trial? Who in Georgia, I demand to know, wants to be tried by a jury like that?" All they asked was for a new trial. Why the rush to hang this boy, he asked.

Mathews issued his ruling the following Wednesday, denying the petition on all counts. "No material or harmful errors" had been made. As for the jurymen, Mathews cited the Georgia precedent that courts will take the sworn oath of a juror in court over what he might have said elsewhere. In closing, Mathews noted that he had been besieged with letters, overwhelmingly from women. "These women do not seem to be able to realize that cases of law cannot be decided on a sympathetic or sentimental basis," he said.

Frank DuPre received the bad news and, maybe for the first time, seemed shaken. He conceded, "Things certainly are looking dark…but I have not given up hope." His attitude recovered quickly. The jailers reported that he was eating well. He was always courteous, kept his cell clean and made his bed daily. Frank was also showing an increasing interest in religion. Preachers visited him regularly and left behind some religious tracts that he had read and found comforting.

There was one visitor he could not see. On March 20, two weeks into her exile to Hall County, Betty Andrews showed up at the Tower demanding to see Frank. She had collected $5.50 on his behalf from people in Gainesville. Judge Humphries was not amused. "I can never conscientiously give you permission to see DuPre," he told her. She had clearly violated her parole, but as she was "an ignorant girl," he would not arrest her this time. "But if you come to Atlanta again, I will have it done." Sheriff's deputies escorted her to the Terminal, where she was "unceremoniously" put on the train to Gainesville.

Not only Humphries but also the public had now lost patience with this troubled girl. In an un-bylined story syndicated nationally, Betty was called a "heartless vampire whose selfishness has brought ruin to herself and to the man she professed to love."[43] The following chart accompanied the article:

What happened when Betty wanted a diamond ring?
A jewelry store was plundered.
One man was murdered.
Another was crippled for life.
A third was sentenced to be hanged.
Two others went to prison.
A wife was widowed.
A baby was made fatherless.
Billy Sunday quarreled with two preachers.
A husband got a divorce.
A whole town was turned topsy-turvy.

Chapter 9

"Insolent Bravado"

The oak-paneled courtroom of the Georgia Supreme Court was a place of "quiet magnificence." On May 16, 1922, it was the setting for the case of *DuPre v. Georgia*.[44] A few blocks away at the Tower, "the appellant" sat on his fold-down cot, smoking.

Allen posited four reasons for a new trial: (1) juror prejudice, (2) technical issues regarding Boykin's counter-affidavits regarding said jurymen, (3) Judge Mathews's instructions to the jury on voluntary manslaughter and (4) the fact that Mathews had failed to make clear to the jury they held unlimited power to recommend mercy, i.e. life in prison.

The court's ruling of July 13 denied the appeal on all counts. On the issue of the impugned jurors and the judge's instructions on manslaughter, the court was unanimous. On the issue of the affidavits, three justices (Fish, Beck and Atkinson) dissented, believing that the prosecution had been too late in submitting theirs. Still, under Georgia law, a court divided 3–3 meant the previous ruling was affirmed.

The court also split 3–3 on the central question of whether Mathews had made it clear to the jurymen that they had absolute authority to recommend life imprisonment. Justice Gilbert thought Mathews left the jurors "free and untrammeled to fix the punishment according to their own will." Gilbert declared that he had rarely read a case where there was so nearly no defense and cited the "insolent bravado" of the letter from the Peachtree Bandit. Gilbert thought the jury instructions were more favorable than the law required.

The dissenting threesome was represented by Justice Hines, who thought Mathews had said too much. It was always best for a judge to simply state the law without elaboration, but Mathews had instructed the jury that it "consider what the object of punishment is, consider all the facts and circumstances of the case, circumstances of mitigation or palliation, or circumstances of aggravation, anything that you think ought to be considered." Hines quoted former justice Little: "Whether [mercy] shall be exercised or not in a capital case is for the jury alone to determine, and the judge may not lawfully abridge this right by instructions which even in the slightest degree qualify its exercise." Justice Atkinson, concurring, said a jury needs no reason at all, that it can grant mercy as "a mere matter of grace." But once again, the court divided 3–3, and thus the appeal failed.

At the Tower, Frank's first thought was to blame the day of the month—he had been captured on the thirteenth of January, and the court turned him down on the thirteenth of July. "They'll probably hang me now on the thirteenth," he laughed. But Frank said he didn't fear death anymore. He planned to read his scriptures and prepare for the end. "I am not afraid to meet my God now that I have been converted."

On the day following the court's ruling, and for the first time in weeks, Betty Andrews lurched back into the news. In Gainesville, she had proven to be too much for her father to control. The Hall County sheriff came to Atlanta pleading that Fulton County take this "undesirable citizen" off their hands. Betty had a new lawyer, Walter Sims, a prominent Klansman and future mayor. Betty was as histrionic as ever; at a hearing on July 18, she was by turns in tears or swooning. She admitted sneaking out of her father's house and taking joyrides with local boys. Her helpless father said that local "rowdies" had besieged their home on the Shallowford Bridge Road. He told Judge Humphries that with Betty's picture being in the papers so much, she had an offer to be a "cloak model" in Chicago. An exasperated Humphries declared, "If she couldn't behave herself in Atlanta and Gainesville, do you think she would do any better in Chicago?" Humphries said she would be placed in the women's farm in Milledgeville, but for the moment, she was sent to the women's ward on the Tower's third floor. Just two floors now separated these luckless lovers, but Betty and DuPre were forbidden to meet or communicate. Frank thought Betty didn't want to see him, and he was offended. "I don't care if I don't see her any more," he said. "I don't care for her now." He was apparently a changed man. "I pray nightly and read my testament."

On Saturday, July 29, Frank was resentenced as required. Judge Humphries's courtroom was full. In the holding cell, shackled and handcuffed, Frank asked that someone comb his hair. His name was called, and he entered with another show of "careless nonchalance." He sat beside the tireless Allen. The process was brief. Humphries ordered DuPre to stand. Frank rose but did not meet the eyes of the judge, looking down at the table. "Have you anything to say before sentence again is pronounced upon you?" the judge asked. Frank replied, "No, sir." Humphries continued, "You were tried by an able and conscientious judge…you were convicted of nothing but murder. I sentence you to be hanged in the common jail of Fulton County on September 1, 1922, between the hours of 10AM and 4PM." Frank showed no emotion; his father wept yet again.

Back at the Tower, Frank held court with reporters. He was always willing to talk in exchange for cigarettes (a "deck" of fifteen cost a dime) or a cold drink. He made clear his dislike for Judge Humphrics. The law required a condemned man be hanged no fewer than twenty and no more than sixty days from sentencing. Frank had expected to get another forty days; instead it was only thirty. "That's ten less days than I figured on," he said. Only thirty-three days remained, and DuPre "seemed more depressed than ever."

Chapter 10

"A Few Thousand Criminal-Worshipping Women"

L et it be clearly understood: the campaign to save Frank DuPre from a rope was driven by the reality that Georgia was about to hang a white boy. There had been no outcry in Augusta, four days before Christmas 1921, when Henry Lacey was arrested, convicted and hanged in little more than twenty-four hours for a sexual assault on a white girl. Lacey was a sixteen-year-old black boy. The story barely made the papers.

As required, the plea for clemency was filed at the courthouse. But much more would be needed, and Frank, his mounting legal bills unpaid, admitted, "We're flat broke." DuPre's father wrote a begging letter to the three newspapers; he thought $2,500 would be enough to save his son. Contributions began arriving at his lodgings on Oglethorpe Avenue in the West End.

The process began on August 10 before the Prison Commission, a three-member board that would make its recommendation to the governor. The small hearing room was filled with familiar faces: Allen, Boykin and their respective supporting counsel. Graham West spoke in opposition to clemency, "not from personal animosity but in the interests of society." In his allotted hour, Allen presented, for the first time, the results of testing by a psychologist who labeled DuPre a "high-grade moron." Allen also delivered boxes of petitions. They survive in the state archives in a collection titled "Governor—Convict and Fugitive Records—Applications for Clemency, 1858–1942."[45] Petitions were not new, but other than the single and celebrated case of Leo Frank, there is no larger record than the appeal of

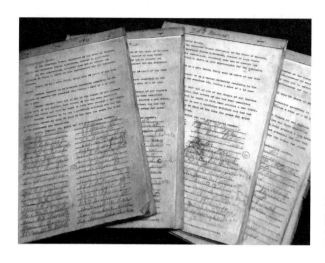

Petitions urging the
governor to commute
DuPre's sentence to life.
Courtesy of the Georgia Archives.

Frank DuPre. The eight folders bulge with now-yellowed petitions with more than twelve thousand signatures.

The petitions had been circulated throughout Atlanta. The signatories "begged" that the governor spare DuPre's life on five grounds:

> *First. DuPre is a mere child, being only nineteen years of age this month.*
> *Second. He is a mental defective according to the opinion of experts who have examined him, having the mind of a thirteen-year-old.*
> *Third. Four out of six judges of our Supreme Court were of the opinion that errors of law had been committed and he ought to have been granted a new trial.*
> *Fourth. He is not a confirmed criminal and had had a criminal career of only 29 days at the time the crime for which he is sentenced and convicted.*
> *Fifth. His crime was not premeditated murder.*

Boykin's deputy, Ed Stephens discounted the effort, saying, "People would sign a petition asking that the sun rise in the west."

The commissioners promised a decision the following morning. That Friday, while his lawyers were at the capitol, Frank was confirmed into the Episcopal Church. The "solemn and impressive" ceremony was held in the jailer's dining room at the Tower. Reverend Russell Smith, from Inman Park's Church of the Epiphany, presented Frank to the Bishop of Atlanta, Reverend Henry Judah Mikell from St. Philip's Cathedral. The prelate, using the *Book of Common Prayer*, asked, "Dost thou renounce the devil and all his works, the vain pomp and glory of the world, with all covetous desires of the same, and the sinful desires of the flesh, so that thou wilt not follow nor be led by them?" Frank replied, "I renounce them all." Bishop Mikell continued, "Almighty and ever living God, who hast vouchsafed to regenerate thy servant by Water and the Holy Ghost, and hast given unto him forgiveness of all his sins…"

Eternal forgiveness may have been vouchsafed, but the news that day from the Prison Commission was crushing. "The appeal of Frank DuPre for executive clemency is denied. The vote was unanimous." Allen tried not to show his disappointment but vowed a "fight to the last ditch." Frank was disappointed and, on a rare occasion, lost his appetite. "I don't feel like eating now," he said. "It's God's will, after all."

The decision was only a recommendation. All the materials were sent to the governor's office. Included were dozens of letters urging the governor to find mercy in his heart for the boy bandit. The vast majority was from women. Far from being the cold-hearted pistol-wielding Don Juan depicted by the prosecution, they saw DuPre as a poor, motherless, slow-witted boy who was a victim of bad connections and a failed society. He had been played for a patsy by a man like Worth. Surely the gallows was not the answer for one so young.

On August 12, there was a brief surge of hope when the *Constitution* quoted Mrs. Walker as saying she would accept clemency if she could be assured that DuPre would never be paroled. But in the *Georgian*, she called the earlier report "absolutely incorrect." She had received hundreds of letters from women, some of them hurtful, but "the normal minded women of this city" believed, as she did, that DuPre should pay the ultimate price for his crime.

Women in Georgia had more than DuPre's case to be concerned with that summer. There was actually a woman on death row. Mrs. Cora Vinson, an Atlanta white woman, had received a death sentence for murdering her husband. Dr. William Vinson was her second husband, but they lived apart. That March, she went to his office to discuss a divorce. She insisted she went with no murderous intent but that when he taunted her that he had found someone younger, she pulled a gun in fury and shot him. In early June, an all-male Fulton County jury convicted her, with no recommendation for mercy.[46] Everyone was dumbfounded. Boykin hadn't asked for the death penalty: "I have never asked a jury to send a woman to the gallows, and I won't begin now." The Vinson sentence shocked the entire country. Sheriff Lowry asserted, "A woman should not be hanged—well, simply because a woman is a woman." But did that view still hold? Women had fought to win the vote. Women were expanding their presence in the business world.

Could they still claim a special "protected" status? Former congressman William Schley Howard, who had helped prosecute Mrs. Vinson, declared, "The women of Georgia, like women of other states, have shown a tendency to come down from this man-created pedestal."[47]

But Mrs. Vinson didn't hang. She appealed, won a new trial and pleaded guilty, receiving a life sentence. But her brief stay in the shadow of the gallows had brought many women forward to publicly question the death penalty. They may have come out of concern for Mrs. Vinson, but many remained to save the doomed "Boy Bandit." One such woman was Mrs. Claud Osburn, an Atlanta neighbor of Mrs. Vinson. Eula Osburn assumed the lead of the loose-knit coalition of women, clergymen, lawyers and journalists (or, as a later Atlanta editor called them, "a crew of emotional, moronic, sob-sisters").[48]

Mrs. Osburn wrote the following to Governor Hardwick: "I never saw anyone in all my life quite so sorry for anything they had done. The first time I went to see him, he told me if he had only had a mother, he would not be in this terrible place. But he had no mother and no home, and, of course, a boy of his age is so easily led astray and he fell in bad company and one of the bunch was a very bad girl, and they were all older than Frank, so you can see how easy it was for them to use him as a 'cat's paw.'"

Mrs. Osburn asked the governor why Jack Worth, who had coached and enabled this naïve boy, got off so lightly. Frank did not get a fair trial. Mrs. Osburn wrote, "The town was at fever heat, the newspapers were full of terrible reports, and even Rev. Ham got up in the pulpit and asked for the death penalty. It was impossible for Frank to get an impartial trial." In the end, she pleaded, "I am just begging you to please spare this poor motherless boy."

Another letter was signed by several prominent Atlanta society women, including Mrs. Price Smith, future president of the Women's Club, and Mrs. Alonzo Richardson, a well-known hostess who chaired Atlanta's Better Films Committee. The signers asked Hardwick to consider DuPre's life story. He had little education, and his mother had gone mad and died when he was fourteen. His "smithy" father followed forges around the South. "Eighteen years of honesty brought [Frank] only poverty, hunger, distress," the letter noted. In a fatal moment, he had stolen from Reville and then again from Davis & Freeman. Then he happened to meet Betty Andrews. "The governor can recall perhaps in his own youth someone he met, under more fortunate circumstances, and the effect of that meeting." Frank was a lovesick boy who had done it all for Betty. "Christmas was nearly at hand. It is December fifteenth. The spirit of the season is infectious. And the young woman expresses a desire for a diamond ring." The women assured the governor that in no way did they diminish the crime; a man had died. But they believed Frank went out that day with no intent to kill Irby Walker, carrying the gun only as a "piece of stage property." But drunk and scared and under ferocious attack, "any boy similarly situated would have acted in just about the same way."

Of course, there were many Georgians who urged their governor to stand firm against such sentimentality. G.M. Green of Ball Ground, for instance, entreated the governor to ignore "a few thousand foolish criminal-worshipping women." Another letter, grandiloquently signed "J.R. English LL.B., S.B," read, "To put it bluntly, there is a lot of the purest bosh going on in DuPre's behalf now."

Chapter 11

"The Life of This Boy"

Thomas Hardwick, Georgia's fifty-first governor, was born in Sandersville in Washington County.[49] He graduated from Mercer and earned a law degree from the University of Georgia. At just twenty-four years old, he became the county prosecutor. Elected to the legislature in 1897, Hardwick made an annual push for a literacy test for voters, which was accurately called the "Negro Disenfranchisement Bill." Hardwick's obsessive hatred of blacks was "distinctly unfashionable" even in Georgia's legislature.[50] But Hardwick attracted the attention of the powerful Tom Watson, the legendary orator and populist. The "Two Toms" were soon a team. With Watson's influence, Hardwick's disenfranchisement bill finally passed, and the number of eligible Negro voters in the state dropped to 5 percent. Hardwick was elected to Congress in 1908.

One contemporary periodical noted, "The Georgia political situation is complicated almost beyond the understanding of an outsider."[51] Hardwick and Watson fell out in 1909. Hardwick remained a congressman until 1914, when he won a special election to fill a U.S. Senate seat. The Great War was on, and Hardwick was a firm isolationist. Stay out of Europe's quarrels, he insisted. Hardwick infuriated his party and President Wilson, who called him a "constant and active opponent of my administration." Back in Georgia, where the war had much greater support, Hardwick was called "Herr Hardwick," supposedly in league with the Kaiser. In 1918, Hardwick lost his bid for a full term in the Senate. In his lame-duck session, as fears of the postwar Red Menace escalated, Hardwick pushed for strict

Governor Thomas W. Hardwick. *Courtesy of the Georgia Archives, Capitol Museum Collection, 1992.23.0057.*

new immigration controls to keep out the Bolsheviks and their ilk. In April 1919, Hardwick was living in Atlanta when a package arrived at his home. The box exploded, burning Mrs. Hardwick and maiming his housekeeper. Hardwick blamed "foreign anarchists." The culprits were never caught.

By 1920, the shifting sands of Georgia politics had brought the "Two Toms" together again. Watson was elected to the U.S. Senate, and Hardwick was elected governor. The rapprochement was short-lived. By the middle of 1922, the Watson and Hardwick forces were bitter enemies again. Watson backed Clifford Walker, who was challenging Hardwick in the Democratic primary that September. Beyond his feud with Watson, Hardwick had surprisingly challenged the powerful Klan.[52] Hardwick was no civil rights leader; he endorsed the Klan's principles and goals. He demanded, however, that the violence of the Klan's "night-riders" must cease and that the hoods and masks must come off. Hardwick was reacting to national newspaper exposés on Klan violence in the South, especially in Georgia. There were calls in Washington to make lynching a federal crime and use the army to put it down. Hardwick said the Klan had to push its agenda by peaceful means and without masks. Reverend Ridley, the Klan Kludd, accused Hardwick of "pussy-footing around with a bunch of loud-lunged moralists and race-mixing men." Hardwick really needed to be out campaigning, and DuPre's appeal was a time-consuming diversion.

So, involved in a bitter fight for his own political life, Hardwick set aside Thursday, August 24, to consider whether he should spare the life of Frank DuPre. The *Georgian* reported that Frank was hopeful: "Everybody just ask God to spare my life, and I'll prove I'm worthy of it."

Hardwick gave each side one hour. The proceedings were held in the capitol's senate chamber. The room, with space for the forty-four senators and staff, was quickly filled. The capitol was infamous for stifling summer conditions, and the windows were wide open. The crowd was predominantly female; they stood waving their fans, in their hats and white gloves, along the brass rail at the rear or peering down from the gallery. Hardwick was seated at the desk of the senate clerk. To his right were the lawyers for the condemned, along with DuPre's father and brother. DuPre was not present; a personal appeal was not permitted. To the governor's left were Boykin, Stephens and the bandit's victims: the widowed Mrs. Walker, her daughter and Mr. and Mrs. West.

Graham West was questioned by the governor at some length about what happened in the Kimball House entryway. West said he had simply turned to look at Frank DuPre, who had fallen behind him. As he turned, DuPre shot him in the face. "It is a miracle I am alive today," he said. West, who labored to control his emotions, admitted it was "extremely unpleasant" to ask for a man's life but that if the governor were to commute the sentence, he would "commit no greater blow to law and order." Mrs. Walker did not speak.

Boykin assured the governor that DuPre's case had been reviewed by the highest court in Georgia and his appeal denied on all counts. There was nothing now but maudlin appeals for sympathy. Boykin said that the newly found defense psychologist was well meaning but had proved nothing other than the fact that DuPre was uneducated. Few criminals were. He referred the governor instead to the findings of the well-respected Dr. Eskridge, who had pronounced DuPre mentally sound. Looking around at "these good women" and churchmen who had come out, the solicitor wondered how many of them had ever visited Mrs. Walker in her grief. "They say he is too young, too dashing, or that he ought not be hanged because he is a mother's boy. Tommyrot! The reason why we have so many murders in this city is that hangings have been scarcer than hen's teeth." Hardwick stopped Boykin to ask if the solicitor knew how many hangings there had been in Georgia in 1922. Boykin admitted he didn't know. "Probably more than you think," said Hardwick. There was a burst of "loud and sustained" applause, but Hardwick rapped for order. Boykin continued, urging the governor to reject "this repentance stunt," adding that when DuPre was asked if he was surprised that he had gotten the death sentence, he responded, "Hell no." Allen leapt to his feet; DuPre never said any such thing. The solicitor knew the laws of hearsay, and Allen demanded he withdraw the statement. There seemed to be a chance of an actual physical confrontation. Hardwick demanded order and reprimanded both of them. Boykin, calmness restored, said his time was now up. Pointing to the piles of petitions, he reminded Hardwick that the great mass of Georgians had not signed any petition: "They consider it beyond reason and comprehension that a murderous highwayman without a single extenuating circumstance should be granted executive clemency. You have no petition from them because the mass of people are taking it for granted that you are going to do your duty. And duty, as Robert E. Lee said, is the sublimest word in the English language."

Allen rose, for the last time, to speak for Frank DuPre. He introduced several clergyman and citizens, the former all male and the latter predominantly women. When Allen began to raise the legal issues in the case, the governor cut him off. "That's been decided," he said. "Confine yourself to why the sentence is unnecessarily severe." Allen said it was the simple injustice of the whole process. In haste, whipped along by a rabid press, the authorities in Fulton County were hell-bent on hanging a mere boy with the mind of a ten-year-old.

Allen then introduced Miss Newell Mason.[53] She had a degree from Macon's Wesleyan Conservatory and advance degrees from the University of

Chicago and Columbia University. In July, Miss Mason met with Frank at the Tower and gave him two tests. On the routine Stanford-Binet IQ test, he scored 80.7, which she described as the score of a "high-grade moron." She had then given Frank a second test, her own creation, the Mason Test of Moral Judgment.[54] Frank was handed a booklet with thirty multiple-choice questions requiring a "what would you have done?" answer. After an hour, Frank had answered only twenty questions. Following are two sample questions:

> *You are a poor married man and your wife is ill. You find a woman's purse. The woman's name is in the purse. You might return it to her and receive a small reward. There is money in the purse. What would you do?* [Frank checked "Keep the purse and use the money for his wife's medical care."]

> *You are a hungry schoolboy. A friend brings you an apple he says he stole from a store. What should you do?* [Frank checked "I could eat the apple in good conscience because I hadn't stolen it."]

Miss Mason stated that she believed DuPre was feebleminded and incapable of competing on equal terms with his peers. He was no match for "the bunch of crooks that had him under their influence." Moreover, he was singularly unfit in matters pertaining to women. Getting involved with Betty Andrews, "who is herself a moron," was a recipe for tragedy. "In a nut shell, he is a morally irresponsible boy, allowed by a negligent society to go around unguarded and uncontrolled—wreaking vengeance on the society that had neglected him and was thus accessory to the murder." He should be in a mental hospital, not in prison, she contended. "I believe that he considers himself the hero of a very thrilling tale of adventure and he would be rather disappointed if he were not hung [*sic*]." (When Frank read the account of Miss Mason's comments, he joked with reporters, "She asked me a lot of foolish questions. If I am a moron, I am not conscious of it and it doesn't seem to hurt me any.")

Allen urged the governor to study Miss Mason's presentation. They were not claiming insanity but that DuPre was "mentally deficient." The state had portrayed him as some daring, master criminal, but in reality, he was a gullible boy cruelly used by evil associates. "I do not say that this boy ought to have yielded to the temptation to steal, but I do say that he had no greater strength than the strength which God gave him and I do say that God, in his mysterious wisdom, gave him less strength of mind and character than he needed." In conclusion, Allen asked the governor to ignore the rush to the gallows. Would not a life sentence suffice? "The constitution of this State gives the governor a power that is comparable only to the divine power… Society, your Excellency, has no right to demand the life of this boy."

The weekend intervened. Hardwick promised his decision by Monday. On Sunday, the twenty-seventh, Frank had something of a treat. That new invention, the radio, was brought into the Tower. That March, the *Journal* launched the city's first radio station, WSB, from the top of its building on Forsyth Street. Sheriff Lowry had allowed a radiophone to be set up in a private room where Frank, his father and brother joined "the invisible congregation" listening to a broadcast from Peachtree's First Presbyterian Church. That afternoon, Frank returned for an hour of sacred music sung by the Reverend DeBardeleben's choir at Payne Memorial Methodist Church. The *Journal* scored the exclusive, of course, with a rather posed photograph showing Frank sitting by the "loud speaker horn." Frank showed an "intense interest" in the new technology and asked numerous questions. Still, the report somberly concluded, "Unless the law's decree is stayed, DuPre's first radio sermons and singing will be his last."

Did Frank have any reason for hope? When Hardwick asked Boykin if he knew how many hangings there were in Georgia, Boykin had no answer. While Boykin may have seemed flippant, in truth, no one knew. The state kept no official count. There were twenty-three judicial circuits in 158 counties, and the state constitution empowered each court to pronounce death sentences and carry them out. Estimates vary, but a reasonable number of legal hangings would be 150 in the years between 1900 and 1922—more than any other state. This figure does not include lynchings. Most hangings didn't even make the Atlanta papers. The records of these uncounted hangings are "scattered throughout a myriad of county, prison and newspaper files that have yet to be examined."[55] The attention paid to Frank DuPre's case was unparalleled for the time.

The number of clemency cases that crossed a governor's desk was startling. In 1922, Hardwick had heard several, and a review either shows him to be a reasonable man or merely demonstrates the randomness of it all.

On June 15, he refused to commute the sentence for Jim Denson, a "negro plow boy" who assaulted a white woman. Denson had already survived one lynching.

On the last day of June, the governor postponed the death sentences of two black farm workers, Joe Jordan and James Harvey, convicted of

UNDER SHADOW OF GALLOWS FRANK DUPRE HEARS FIRST SERMON OVER RADIOPHONE

FRANK DuPRE, SENTENCED TO HANG NEXT FRIDAY for the murder of Detective Irby C. Walker, listening to radio for the first time. He heard the First Presbyterian church morning service and The Journal's sacred program Sunday afternoon. The re-

A Sunday with the radio. Atlanta Journal, *August 28, 1922.*

raping their white employer's wife. The newly formed NAACP and "several prominent white women in Wayne County" brought new evidence forward, and Hardwick granted a thirty-day respite. The Wayne County sheriff replied, "Your order received with much sorrow." The following day, Harvey and Jordan were taken from the jail by "a mob" and lynched.

On July 6, Hardwick did a rather extraordinary thing—he overruled the prison board and commuted to life the sentence of John Thompson, a black man who killed a white night watchman in Clarke County.

On July 21, Hardwick commuted to life the death sentence of Voge Lamar, a black gambler who killed a "Negress" during a card game shootout.

Finally, and just two days before DuPre's hearing, the governor commuted the sentence of a brutal child killer whose crime had convulsed southwest Georgia. Glen Hudson, a white farmer near Albany, was convicted of killing his wife's two illegitimate children, fathered by another man. The boys had eaten some forbidden watermelon. Hudson had beaten them with a stick and fired separate "pistol shots to the head." This was another Georgia case impacted by the curious state rule that a wife could not testify against her husband. The prosecution relied entirely on circumstantial evidence. Hudson's wife made a tearful appeal for his life. Hardwick's decision was not a popular one.

Hardwick spent the weekend doing the barbecue campaign circuit through the mountains of northeast Georgia. On Monday, his office announced that the decision on the DuPre case would take another day. Frank was now receiving communion daily. His supporters gathered outside his cell. "In utter disregard of physical discomfort, these people who seem so sincere in their belief that the life of this boy should be spared knelt on the bare cement floor and prayed," reported one paper. Communion was brought by the Reverend George Gasque of Holy Comforter Episcopal Church on Pulliam Street.

On Tuesday morning, Hardwick's written response was ready: no reprieve, no respite, no clemency. As for Miss Mason's claim that DuPre was some kind of moron, Hardwick believed that could "probably be said of a vast majority of criminals." Despite his youth, DuPre's actions in the killing of Irby Walker and the wanton shooting of Graham West showed his "desperate determination to slay as many human beings as was necessary to escape apprehension." Again, the "boneheads" letter haunted DuPre's hopes. Hardwick said the note "breathes of bravado and a reckless disregard of human life that is appalling and terrifying." The fugitive bandit had "gloated over his deeds of theft and murder," and "his only repentance came when he was in the clutches of the law."

Hardwick acknowledged the prayers, letters and appeals he had received from so many "tender-hearted persons." His heart had been touched as well, but there were others in his thoughts: "What of the faithful, law-abiding man, Mr. Walker, who sleeps in an untimely grave? What of the little woman who is widowed by his act? What of the seven-year-old orphan? If DuPre was motherless, he left a little girl fatherless."

Hanging DuPre, the governor hoped, would be a deterrent to others: "Unless our boys, who may even now have embarked on a similar path to that pursued by this applicant, who may be filling themselves with cheap and poisonous liquor, who may be associating with gamblers and prostitutes, are checked in their mad courses of crime, who can tell how many orphans will be made in Georgia by their conduct? It is to protect society, to save these other women from being made widows, these other men being slain, those other children from being made orphans that it is necessary—and absolutely necessary—that the supreme penalty of the law be executed upon this applicant."

Hardwick also seized on the DuPre case to reassert the state's sole authority for the ultimate punishment of the law. According to him, DuPre's hanging would be "the most solemn and impressive warning that can be given in the name of the law and in the name of civilized society, and in the name of organized government. Nothing has developed since the trial to in any way affect or alter the case. Guilt is still undisputed, still un-denied and still proven. Under these circumstances, I feel it to be my sworn duty, before God and man, to allow the law to take its course."

Hardwick's decision was largely accepted. The *Georgian* acknowledged, "It would be a hard-hearted citizen indeed who did not feel a measure of melancholy because of the tragic fate that has come to Frank DuPre." It was worth noting that the bandit had received legal counsel that would be the envy of "every criminal in Georgia, high and low, rich and poor, black and white." But the law had spoken. "May God have mercy on [his] Soul." The *Independent*, a black-owned newspaper published by "Big Ben" Davis on Auburn Avenue, praised the governor: "It took a big man to turn down the plea of 25,000 women…DuPre's crime was revolting and he deserves death, but it took a man who could stand up against the sentiment to say, 'Let the law take its course.'"

The most outspoken critic was Tom Loyless, editor of the *Columbus Enquirer-Sun* and a strong foe of the death penalty, who opined, "Is this the best answer civilization can make to crime? Here and there we seek to satisfy our conscience and uphold the majesty of the law by seizing upon some poor devil, some wretch against whom public opinion cries out, and we put him to death 'in order to deter others.' The world will someday look back on the gallows as the ghostly device of a crude civilization."

The gallows, however, now awaited Frank DuPre after but three more sunrises. In his cell, he heard the news stoically. "It is God's will, and I am ready to go." He sat on his cot, smoking cigarettes and chewing gum. A vase with a few asters in water adorned the lone windowsill. In the afternoon, Frank's cell was turned over. The deathwatch had begun, and the guards searched for anything that might be used to cheat the hangman. All visitors were searched. Guards would now watch him until the end.

A second man would also swing on Friday. Luke McDonald, a black man, had been convicted of killing his girlfriend. When he discovered Lizzie Cowan was seeing another man, McDonald went to where she stayed on Piedmont Avenue and demanded she leave with him or he would shoot her dead. She refused. He did. McDonald said he envied all the attention "Mr. DuPre" was getting. "Not much hope for this poor negro with the Governor and all the white folks' mind on poor DuPre. I expect as how they just overlooked me," he said. That mention in the *Georgian* prompted an eleventh-hour review of McDonald's case. Clemency was denied.

Allen used the remaining days for one more novel (or desperate) argument. In *DuPre v. Georgia*, Allen noted that on the affidavits question, three justices supported a new trial: Beck, Fish and Atkinson. On the jury charge question, three justices believed there should be a new trial: Hines, Fish and Atkinson. Therefore, only two of the justices, Gilbert and Hill, were unalterably opposed to a new trial. By that reasoning, Allen claimed that by a 4–2 ruling, there should be a new trial. Allen filed his motion, but Chief Justice Fish, who had actually favored a new trial on both divisions of the court, refused to rehear the case nonetheless.

On Wednesday night, August 30, Allen chased the governor to Carrollton, where he was speaking to the Swine Growers Association. The lawyer begged for a thirty-day reprieve to allow time for a federal appeal on the "4–2 argument." Again, Hardwick would not intervene.

Mrs. Osburn sent a wire to President Harding. On the thirty-first, the president's private secretary replied by telegram stating that Mr. Harding could only communicate his views to Governor Hardwick as a private citizen. The White House had no standing in a purely state matter.

As the hours dwindled, the *Georgian* headlined, "WOMEN FIGHT TO SAVE DUPRE." Mrs. Sam Jones, the widow of a legendary evangelist, a born-again drunken lawyer, sent her appeal to all the Christian women of

Georgia: "Save the life of this motherless boy who was not only subnormal but under the influence of alcohol."

Frank's Thursday seemed fairly routine—to him, anyway. He took communion and prayed with visitors. He gave way to rare tears as he knelt with a Miss Jeannette Jones, a "slender young woman, brunette and pretty."

Fulton County Jail, aka the Tower, 1959. The gallows had been located in the rooftop structure below the radio mast. *Courtesy of the Kenan Research Center, Atlanta History Center.*

She held Frank's hands. For many women, the scene had become too stressful. Frank wrote a farewell letter to one of them:

> *My Dear Mrs.* [Graham] *Perdue—I wish to thank you from the bottom of my heart for the interest you have taken in me and for the work you have done in my behalf; and if God will spare my life, I will certainly try to prove that your kindness towards me is really appreciated. I am not the hardened criminal the papers say. May God bless you and repay you for the kindness extended me; also I am asking that you continue in your prayers for my soul. I beg to remain, Faithfully Yours, Frank DuPre.*

The details of Frank's last hours are complete as newspapermen were allowed to remain and record everything. Fuzzy Woodruff, who had been observing DuPre since his return from Detroit, saw a marked change: "He has aged and seems to have benefited from the good people who have worked with him. You see less of the smiles of part amusement, part pride and part stupidity that doomed him in court." Still, Woodruff observed in DuPre a "Micawberish hope that something will turn up." It was as if DuPre were watching a movie and expecting that someone would ride up with a pardon from the governor to save him. Frank "has been seeing a stirring motion picture, all the more stirring because he has seen himself as the central figure. But always he has seen the foam flecked horse and the road stained horseman and the great seal and the happy fade out."

Thursday night, Allen paid one last visit to the governor at the Georgian Terrace hotel, the temporary governor's mansion. It was a visit in vain. Allen confided to a reporter that it was over.

By midnight, small groups began gathering in the darkened streets outside the Tower. They could be heard praying. Some claimed they could hear inmates within singing hymns, a notable event considering the Tower held "the hardest criminals in the city." A sheriff's deputy announced that the gallows had been thoroughly greased and tested. The rope had been stretched with a weighted sandbag. All was in readiness.

Chapter 12

"That's Some Crowd, Isn't It?"

F rank DuPre rose at seven o'clock on Friday morning, September 1, 1922. A new day began; around him the commonplace sullen din of guards and inmates, shouts and curses, went on. Frank had slept well. After a bath, he dressed in his gray suit, supposedly the one he wore the day of the shooting. He had given his infamous "gray overcoat" to brother Joe.

The newspapermen were in place: the *Constitution*'s Fuzzy Woodruff, the *Journal*'s Rogers Winter and the un-bylined correspondent for the *Georgian*. Melding the three accounts gives a clear chronology to the somber process.

Frank's father and brother arrived at 7:45 a.m., sitting with him while he picked at his breakfast of ham, eggs, toast, French-fried potatoes and coffee. Frank seemed composed. In fact, the reporters all agreed that, unlike his visitors, Frank evidenced the least obvious distress.

At 8:00 a.m., two "colored" clergymen arrived at the Tower to sit and pray with McDonald, the condemned Negro. Reverend C.D. Thornton from Flipper Temple AME Church paused at Frank's cell to say, "We have been praying for you the same as for our colored brother in yonder. Be brave young man." Through the bars, the white man and the black preacher shook hands.

At 9:00 a.m., attorneys Allen and Foster paid a final call. Frank thanked them both, saying, "You have done everything you could. You have fought a brave fight." With emotion, Allen replied, "Yes, but I failed, Frank. There is nothing more on earth to be done." They withdrew.

Frank had a final communion service; Reverend Gasque presided, assisted by clergymen of various Protestant faiths. Interestingly, Frank's religious support network did not include Catholics or Jews, alien faiths in the South. A small "congregation" stood outside the cell, including Mr. DuPre, Joe and women, many of them weeping. The few women admitted represented the "hundreds" of Atlanta women, the Associated Press reported, "anxiously expectant and with immovable faith" united in prayer. Mrs. Osburn arrived, her eyes red from an all-night vigil at Mr. DuPre's lodgings.

The service ended at 10:35 a.m., and Frank's father could take it no longer. "I cannot stand it." He hugged Frank through the bars and urged him to "be brave." He left in tears; his final words were, "I'll see you sometime."

Throughout the Tower, there was a pall. The deputies moved about making preparations. The wings echoed with inmates singing hymns and shouting scripture verse. Outside, the crowd grew larger on Butler Street despite the late summer heat. It was "the hottest day of the summer." At the Lakewood Fairgrounds, the Yaarab Temple summer picnic was getting started. The Civitan Club held its luncheon, presumably attended by Graham West. The talk of the nation was the end of the great railroad strike. On Butler Street, Chief Beavers's mounted police kept the roadway clear. Trucks servicing the jail with ice, laundry and such came and went. The crowd parted respectfully when two funeral vans arrived. One came from Poole's Chapel on Pryor Street to await the bandit's remains. McDonald's body would go to Howard's Funeral Home on Piedmont, founded by a former slave.

Such routine comings and goings were all the "excitement" the scene afforded. There was nothing to see. It has been claimed that Frank's was the "last public hanging in Georgia." Public hangings—at least the judicially sanctioned ones—had stopped as far back as 1893.[56] Frank would hang behind the looming granite walls of the Tower. The gallows were on the fifth floor. High above the street, there was a single small barred window that gave the condemned a final glimpse of the world being left behind. Anytime a figure moved past that window, shouts went up from Butler Street.

The crowd, if "morbidly curious," was quiet and respectful. They were of "every race, every color, every social and financial degree." Rooftop vantage points were prized; a few people were seen in the gallery of the capitol dome. At noon, everyone jumped when the whistle from the nearby Atlanta Milling Company shrieked to announce midday. A persistent drizzle began falling.

Reverend Ridley, the Klan preacher, came to offer his final blessing. No doubt, he scored the governor for his refusal to commute the sentence.

And what of Betty Andrews? At the last, Sheriff Lowry allowed her to write a note: "Dear Frank—I am trying so hard to be brave because you asked me to. I am trusting in God. He knows best. I will be good, and I will lead a Christian life. Lovingly, Betty." Frank, his coolness gone, pleaded in vain for one final meeting with the woman for whom he had done it all. He was told that the elevator bringing him to the fifth floor was an open metal cage and that he'd be able to see Betty as he rode up.

A last lunch, prepared by friends, arrived, but the fried trout, creamed potatoes, stewed corn and corn muffins went uneaten. Frank said, politely, "I don't want it—just coffee and a piece of pie." The early editions of the afternoon papers were brought in. The headline "DUPRE TO HANG TODAY" was hard to miss.

At 12:30 p.m., Lowry ordered everyone out but those authorized to attend the gallows. Only Frank's brother, Reverend Gasque and Reverend Robert Tyler of the Methodist Council remained. Several women became "hysterical." Miss Jones began screaming and hitting her head and was carried away. Mrs. Osburn assured Frank that his case would help put an end to the barbarous death penalty. Frank said, "Yes, it probably will."

At 1:00 p.m., McDonald was taken from his cell. He had been waiting with the ministers of his race. They sang the Negro spiritual "God Be with You till We Meet Again." His last meal was a bag of grapes. The news accounts of the day focused on Frank's execution. The *Constitution* noted briefly that McDonald "died bravely."

The gallows had to be reset. The trapdoor spring needed to be reengaged. A new rope would be required, previously stretched with a weighted sandbag to prevent a yo-yo-like snapback. The noose had to be tied at the exact location to allow the "drop" to break the neck. Traditionally, the U.S. Army formula was employed, and the weight of the clothed condemned was divided into 1,020 to arrive at a drop in feet.[57] If Frank weighed, as reported, 130 pounds, a drop of seven and a half feet was needed. At 1:40 p.m., all was ready. Lowry returned to the first floor and told Frank it was time. He walked steadily to the elevator cage.

As the elevator squeaked and whined slowly up the four floors to the gallows, Betty and DuPre, the twosome at the center of months of tragedy and legal wrangling, saw each other for the last time. They had been kept apart from the day Frank was brought back from Detroit. It was a brief vertical meeting. As promised, she was there as Frank ascended past "West Third." It wasn't but a moment, but Frank gave a shackled wave as the lift went past, shouting out, "I'll see you in heaven." Betty was shrieking uncontrollably. She would be good, she sobbed. She would pray for him. Then, Frank rose out of sight.

On the fifth floor, Frank walked down the corridor, passing the barred window overlooking Butler Street. He stopped to look out. A voice in the crowd shouted, "There he is!" The crowd, now in the thousands, began calling his name. The "cold nerve of the boy…was like an electrical touch to the crowd below," reported the *Georgian*. "They could not hold themselves as they rushed forward to bid good bye and God speed to the unfortunate boy." Frank turned to his brother and said, "Gee, Joe, what a crowd. That's some crowd, isn't it?" Frank seemed "utterly pleased," noted the *Journal*. Then Frank began waving and yelling "Good-Bye," though surely no one could hear him. Deputy Sheriff Jim Bazemore, a "gigantic man," gently moved Frank along the hallway. The people saw him no more.

At 1:50 p.m., Frank climbed the wooden steps. The purpose-built gallows had been added when the Tower was constructed in 1898. The noose was "fastened to an iron bolt which connects with a crossbeam up in the roof of an alcove made for the purpose and which is several feet above the main roof of the building." Joe DuPre climbed to the platform with him. Joe shook his brother's hand and broke down. He was helped away. Bazemore, as required, read out the official death warrant. A last hymn, chosen by Frank, was sung. "My Mother's Prayers Have Followed Me" was a Billy Sunday favorite:

> *I'm coming home, I'm coming home,*
> *To live my wasted life anew.*
> *For mother's prayers have followed me,*
> *Have followed me the whole world through.*

Though all made a manful effort, the voices were "unintelligible." Reverend Gasque read the *Book of Common Prayer*'s passages for those about to die: "Unto God's gracious mercy and protection we commit thee. The Lord bless thee, and keep thee. The Lord lift up His countenance upon thee, and give thee peace, both now and evermore." The *Constitution*'s Woodruff noted that during the prayers, Frank stood looking at the gallows "as if they were a piece of motion picture scenery." When Gasque finished, Frank said in a clear voice, "I'm going to heaven." Gasque replied, "I'm sure of it, Frank." Then the clergyman moved down the gallows steps.

The moment had come. Frank was asked to step forward. The deputies, using hemp rope, "speedily and neatly lashed his arms against his body and his knees against each other." As the noose was slipped over his head, his hair was knocked into his eyes. Frank, "a dude to the last," in Franklin Garrett's words,[58] asked that someone brush his hair back. Deputy Sheriff Smith obliged. The "tight-fitting and ghastly" black cap went over Frank's head, more to spare the witnesses. The knot of the noose was adjusted to the recommended position, below Frank's left ear, where it would most efficiently break the neck. A muffled voice was heard: "Good-bye Mr. Smith, Good-bye Sheriff, Good-bye all."

Sheriff Lowry, from the rear of the gallows, threw the lever at 2:04 p.m. Woodruff noted, "Suddenly, there sounded in the deathly silence a metallic clang." Frank was left to hang from 2:04 until 2:21, an "unusually long" time. The body "twitched horribly." Grady Hospital's Dr. Folsom, ironically the same doctor who had pronounced Irby Walker dead 260 days prior, found life extinct. The noose was cut, and the black cap was removed. The undertakers from Poole's placed the body in their wicker basket. A gray vehicle left the Tower gates, and the crowd outside parted silently as the driver headed for the chapel on Pryor Street.

It was over. Winter, the *Journal*'s observer, credited DuPre with showing "more coolness, more nerve, more composure, and more impersonal abstraction that any of the witnesses." It was that stolidity that the *Constitution*'s Woodruff could not fathom. He wrote that DuPre died the "mental enigma" he had been all along. But the *Georgian*'s observer adjudged that DuPre's abiding calmness was "almost uncanny in its inclination toward cheerfulness." Again, why was he smiling?

Governor Hardwick was speaking in Bainbridge when the lever was pulled. He made no reference to the events in Atlanta other than his usual pledge to uphold law and order in Georgia.

In Atlanta, there was a private service at Poole's. Frank's father and brother were joined by the women and clergy who had worked on Frank's behalf. Reverend Tyler, impressed by Frank's peace at the end, spoke. "If I can feel as safe about the hereafter as Frank did when my time comes, I will be contented," he said. The body was placed aboard an evening Seaboard train for Abbeville.

At about 1:30 on Saturday morning, despite the hour, "a large number" of friends and relatives formed a somber welcoming party in Abbeville. The body was taken to the home of Frank's uncle, James Cox, on Lemon Street. At noon, there was a viewing in the living room. Frank's "face was calm in death; a small dark place underneath the chin, the only mark." A constant stream of people called. A short service was led by a Baptist minister, Reverend Horace Weeks. "By special request," Miss Fannie Stark and Miss Vic Howie sang again the last hymn Frank had heard on earth, "My Mother's Prayers." The last journey was the short distance to the cemetery. "Few cemeteries in South Carolina can rival Upper Long Cane Cemetery for its association with, and ability to convey, the history of a town, its county,

The DuPre graves in Abbeville's Upper Long Cane Cemetery. *Photo by author.*

its region."[59] A simple service was held. "The newly made grave was covered with flowers and no sign of earth could be seen." Most of the floral tributes had come from Atlanta. Frank was buried beside his mother. After Frank's father died in 1925, a new and larger stone was placed to mark the graves of Frank A. and Frank B. DuPre.

In Atlanta, DuPre's death brought closure to an exhausting ordeal. The general reaction was that the hanging was well deserved, but as the *Macon Telegraph* conceded, some "public moaning" was understandable, owing to the bandit's youth. The *Columbus Enquirer-Sun*, led by the relentless Loyless, waited until Sunday morning to scold those who had sought to "crucify" Frank DuPre: "They may all go to church today—it's a fine day for churchgoing—and sing and pray and praise God that they are 'not as other men are.' And they ought to thank God too that He let them hang Frank DuPre and that Frank isn't here to enjoy this glorious September Sunday." The *Savannah Morning News* decried the "remarkable attitude of some women." The *Athens Banner* thought Hardwick was "to be commended by all law-abiding and law-respecting people in this state."

Atlanta moved on, titillated by a juicy scandal involving Walter Candler, scion of the Coca-Cola family, who had supposedly seduced another man's wife on a cruise to Europe. Meanwhile, the day after DuPre had been hanged, there was a lynching in Winder. A black man was accused of beating a white woman during a break-in. Barrow County deputies were moving the suspect to Atlanta for his safety when a mob "overpowered" them. Jim Long was hanged from a tree and shot. According to a news account, "the lynching was conducted in an orderly manner and no more trouble is anticipated."

Chapter 13

The Last Man to Hang in Georgia (Not)

On September 13, Governor Hardwick suffered a crushing defeat at the polls, carrying only 42 of 156 counties. In Fulton County, he took less than 40 percent of the vote. The Watson forces were delighted, as was the Klan. Ridley claimed that Hardwick had promised him that DuPre wouldn't hang, but the governor "got so mixed up with the inter-racial gang" that he was compelled to refuse clemency. "DuPre's execution was a political play which was resented by nine tenths of the voters of Georgia," said Ridley. Hardwick, even in defeat, fired back, denouncing the Klan Kludd as a "charlatan and a blatherskite." The idea that he ever promised Ridley anything was "an absolute and willful falsehood. The man is absolutely without character or veracity."

Ridley aside, many believed that the DuPre decision hurt Hardwick, especially among women. The year 1922 was the first in which Georgia women could vote. James Nevin, in his "Sidelights on Georgia Politics" column in the *Georgian*, reported getting a postcard with the following note written in a feminine hand: "When Governor Hardwick permitted Frank DuPre to hang, he sacrificed 50,000 votes of Georgia women." Nevin scoffed, "Asking the lady's pardon, I do not believe it." The point might also be made that while Hardwick lost votes in Atlanta because he allowed DuPre to be hanged, he lost votes in south Georgia because they didn't hang Hudson, the child killer.

So, the question must be asked: why was it so necessary that Frank DuPre be hanged?

Firstly, he killed a man, a law enforcement officer. But it was argued that Frank had no intention to kill anyone. In Georgia, murder was murder, requiring no premeditation. The penalty was death. It was true that jurymen were not unreasonable, but this was no crime of passion. This was the wanton killing of a married man and a father doing his job by a young drunken gunman trying to steal a diamond ring.

Should Frank have been spared the gallows on the grounds that he was a "high-grade moron?"[60] After all, it could be said that it was Frank's limited intellect, not police work, that led to his arrest. Sending the pawn ticket to Silverman when Frank had every opportunity to know that the ring was gone was incomprehensible. But stupidity—call it naïveté or innocence—is no defense. Georgia's prisons were filled with such men. Frank was not insane; he heard no voices, nor did he act out in any way. In fact, he had shown some nascent signs of criminal talent. He was smart enough to change his clothes after the robbery, calling it an act of "common sense." He plotted a multi-state flight to elude the police. Once in custody, he was quite well spoken. He clearly understood right from wrong.

Frank's body language and smirking visage at his trial certainly cost him dearly with the jury. As Woodruff wryly noted, Frank never quite came up to the mark on "his histrionic duty to appear sad and penitent." The press accounts failed to miss a single smirk. The more witnesses to something, the more believable the accounts. If the reporters saw it, the jurymen did also. DuPre, when not semi-grinning, sat impassively. Did that convey an unfeeling coldness? Given his single chance to alter that impression, he dropped the ball. His failure to utter a few simple words of regret or repentance cost him his life. But such repentance would always be contrasted with the celebrated "boneheads" letter. Up to the time of his arrest, Frank was quite pleased with himself, enjoying his self-declared title of the Peachtree Bandit. That letter, replete with "insolent bravado," sent Frank to the noose. Any man who could write such a defiant letter, vowing revenge on those who had helped the police, was not deserving of merciful consideration.

At the simplest level, of course, Frank DuPre was an example. The death penalty has always been justified for having a deterrent effect. There is the old English case in which the condemned man said to the judge, "M'lord, it's rather hard that I'm going to hang for stealing one lousy sheep." To which the judge replied, "I see that you don't understand. You will hang to discourage others from stealing sheep."[61]

As for Governor Hardwick, he might have granted clemency at little political cost. But Hardwick needed a case to demonstrate that the orderly processes of justice could still work in Georgia. The governor's back had stiffened after July's tragic double lynching in Wayne County. The DuPre case was suited to show to all that a criminal, even a white one, can be captured, tried, found guilty, have his full legal appeals heard and—when justified—be hanged. Rejecting DuPre's appeal, Hardwick made that point specifically: "It is to give to them and to all in this state and throughout this country the most solemn and impressive warning that can be given in the name of the law and in the name of civilized society, and in the name of organized government." So let it be done.

———·•·———

The first meeting of the League for the Abolition of Capital Punishment in Georgia was held on October 5. Mrs. Osburn presided, and Reverend DeBardeleben spoke. What deterrence, he asked? Georgia's murder rate remained shockingly high; capital punishment had "failed utterly to do what it is intended to do." The randomness of it all was cruel. "One jury will hang a man, while another, according to the same evidence, will not." The league would seek a new law establishing what we now know as life without parole. The press labeled the new group the Anti-Noose League. At that year's Southeastern Fair, league members handed out literature and took signatures on a petition. The early response was encouraging, and a bill was ready for the 1923 legislative session.

Of course, the league was running far ahead of most Georgians. The Tabernacle's Reverend Ham, for instance, derided such "well-meaning misguided sentimentalists" and their "idle iridescent dream." He predicted that the "virtue of every white woman in Georgia" would be in jeopardy. "As long as we have the Negro in the South, and the vicious white man, so long will we need to safeguard our womanhood and law abiding citizens with the protection that capital punishment alone affords," he said. Ham did concede that the noose was barbaric, and he prayed that Georgia would join those states using the "instantaneous and humane" electric chair.

In 1923, a bill was introduced in the statehouse to make life in prison the maximum punishment. The co-sponsors were an unlikely pair. Viola Napier of Macon, Georgia's first female legislator, was joined by Atlanta's Joe Wood, one of several newly elected Klan-backed candidates. As expected, the "iridescent dreams" met reality, and the repeal effort was easily crushed. There was a growing consensus, however, that some reform was needed. County by county hangings had become insupportable. The lack of security, coupled with the open complicity of local authorities, led to numerous lynchings. The state needed to take control of executions in one central secure location, employing the electric chair. By the 1924 session, the only question was where. Milledgeville, already home to the largest prison farm, was chosen. The "chair" (built by inmates) was made ready, over the objections of Senator J. Howard Ennis, who thought the executions would "create a morbid atmosphere" for the students of the nearby Georgia College. Four weeks later, Howard Hinton, a black male, was electrocuted for a Dekalb County murder. The chair was eventually moved to the new state prison in remote Reidsville.

It is frequently stated that Frank DuPre was the "last man to hang in Georgia." That is simply not true. He was not even the last man to hang in Atlanta. He was not even the last white man to hang in Atlanta. James Satterfield hanged in the Tower on May 23, 1924, for the murder of his brother-in-law. Satterfield left a note hoping that he would be the last man to hang in the Tower, but that would not be the case either. On May 18, 1926, "the final chapter in the annals of Fulton County's criminal gallows history" was written with the hanging of Mack Wooten. A "one-eyed negro ex-con," Wooten had murdered wealthy Atlanta lumberman Dan Williams. Wooten had been indicted before the electrocution statute was passed. A court ruled that he had to be hanged. The gallows were rebuilt. In February 1927, the Tower gallows were dismantled and the "gruesome equipment" removed forever.

On June 12, 1931, Arthur Meyers, a black man who murdered a white policeman, was hanged in Augusta. The murder had occurred in 1924, before the chair came into use. Seven years later, Meyers was truly "the last legal execution by hanging" in Georgia.[62] For those who have the interest, the hood, noose and rope from Meyers's execution can be found in the Augusta Museum of History. Look for them in the Curiosity Corner.

Chapter 14

Mrs. Walker, the Ghost of Frank DuPre and Mrs. Blaustein

There are a few loose ends to the Peachtree Bandit story.

It took the wisdom of a Fulton County judge to divide the $1,955 reward fund. The Detroit police shared $1,000, Chief Hackett in Chattanooga received $400, the clerk at Childs Hotel got $190 and Albert Belle Isle received $50. The wily pawnbroker Max Silverman got a few hundred bucks, but he probably lost money dealing with "John Doe."

The Jewelry Protective Association had contributed a rather chary $100 to the fund. The JPA applauded the efforts of the Pinkerton forces to bring the killer to justice. A Pinkerton executive estimated the agency spent more than $5,000 in the pursuit and prosecution of Irby Walker's killer.

No Pinkerton official was quite as open about the money the agency spent stubbornly fighting the survivor's benefit the state awarded to his widow. The commissioner of the Georgia Department of Commerce and Labor decreed that Mrs. Walker should receive ten dollars a week for three hundred weeks, paid by Pinkerton, under the Employer's Liability Act. It took two years and the Georgia Supreme Court to get the widow her money. Pinkerton attorneys argued that Walker did not die as a result of his employment because DuPre did not know that the man he was struggling with was a Pinkerton detective. The unanimous court found to the contrary that "the undisputed facts show that Walker was killed in the course of his employment because of the employment. The argument in its strongest light is that if Walker had not been employed he would not have been killed." Mrs. Walker used her money to purchase a boardinghouse in Montgomery.[63]

If John Boykin thought the exemplary use of some "good old-fashioned rope" would prove a deterrent, the murder statistics surely frustrated him. In 1925, Atlanta remained second only to Memphis in murders per capita. Boykin sent several more men to the new electric chair, remaining Fulton County's lead prosecutor until his retirement in 1945. At his death in 1948, Boykin was eulogized as the "nemesis of crime" and a crusading "enemy of the underworld."

DuPre's dogged counsel, Henry Allen, crossed swords with Boykin many more times. He defended Alvin Merritt, the so-called Northside Fiend. Boykin sent Merritt to the chair in 1929. When Allen died in 1946, the *Constitution* wrote that "it was often said that he was always on the losing side, but his record actually shows many acquittals, and frequently against great odds."

Tom Hardwick's time as a lame-duck governor was eventful. After Senator Watson's death in late September, Hardwick created a national stir when he named eighty-seven-year-old Rebecca Felton to serve until a special election could be held. Felton is a remarkable historical footnote as the first female U.S. Senator and the last former slaveholder to sit in that body. Hardwick was accused of pandering to Georgia's new female voters. If that was his intent, it didn't succeed. In November, he lost a bid to fill Watson's seat. Hardwick never held elective office again, returning to private law practice. He died in 1944.

Frank's father never recovered from the tragedy. He remained briefly in Atlanta, unemployed and unrecognized. Francis A. DuPre died in 1925. He was only forty-five.

Around the time of the first anniversary of Frank DuPre's hanging, a Tower inmate saw his ghost. Howard Wright was in Frank's old cell and told the *Sunday Journal* that the spirit had been coming around for a few weeks. "I want to talk to him, but I can't muster up enough courage," he said. He tried offering a cigarette. The ghost was smartly dressed, in the same suit of clothes that DuPre wore to the gallows. His hair was neatly combed, and he wore a "stoical" expression. Wright figured that Frank was looking for Betty Andrews. He told him she'd gone. A nearby inmate told the reporter that Wright was crazy. All his ghost talk had done was stir up the superstitious black inmates, who were now singing songs and burning candles all night to keep the ghost away.[64]

When the shade of Frank DuPre came in search of Betty Andrews, she had been gone from Atlanta for some time. Without fanfare, Betty was released from the Tower in early October 1922, paroled in the custody of a "motherly old lady," a widowed former schoolteacher, Mrs. Jessie Dennis, who lived in the Kirkwood section. Alas, Betty's inability to live quietly surfaced again. Neighbors complained that she was out at all hours, walking in her bedroom slippers and other "unconventional attire." The locals heckled her. Mrs. Dennis, "her eyes flaming," charged that the poor girl was being persecuted and denounced the "lying tongues" of her neighbors. But Judge Humphries wearily thundered, "I thought I was releasing her to a minister. If no one can care for this girl, I must send her to the farm."

Betty was returned to the Tower in tears but released three days later in custody of the Reverend Gasque, who had stood with Frank on the gallows. The clergyman assured the court, "She is not immoral by nature. She simply lacks that depth of character and thought which is necessary for a girl that faces the obstacles which met Betty Andrews." He would seek a school for Betty, "out west" somewhere, "to which the notoriety attendant on her exciting past has not penetrated." Gasque hoped that she might anonymously "begin again the normal life of a young girl."

We can report that the kindly hopes of Reverend Gasque, at least for anonymity, were satisfied. On August 2, 1932, a decade removed from the DuPre tragedy and signing her childhood name, Peggy Guest, to the registry, Betty was married in Hot Springs, Arkansas, to Maurice Blaustein. For marrying a non-Jew, Blaustein was disowned by his family. He was a career military supply officer. The 1940 census shows the Blausteins at Fort Meade, Maryland, with six-year-old Robert Blaustein. The youth came from a broken home and, though never formerly adopted, took the Blaustein name. The family moved regularly from post to post, even spending some time in Atlanta in 1943.[65] Robert never heard Margaret, as he knew her, ever talk about Frank DuPre.[66] In the 1950s, Major Blaustein and Margaret retired to Amarillo, Texas. She died there on June 27, 1972, at the age of sixty-eight. Robert Blaustein had clashed with his foster mother even into his adulthood and shed no tears at her passing.[67] The woman once called a "lynx-eyed paramour" and "heartless vampire" was mourned as a member of the Beautiful Saviour Lutheran Church, survived by her husband and her sister, Hazel.[68]

Chapter 15

"Betty Tol' DuPre"

On September 6, 1922, the *Atlanta Journal* published a photograph of a man holding up a copy of the newspaper's edition from the day of the hanging. The headline read, "'MEET ME IN HEAVEN' DUPRE SHOUTS TO GIRL ON WAY TO GALLOWS." The man pictured was "blind radio poet" Andy Jenkins.[69] The legend of Betty and DuPre was underway.

Jenkins was thirty-seven. Born in rural Butts County and blinded since childhood due to a medication error, he was raised in a Pentecostal family. By his teen years, "Blind Andy" was a popular stump preacher. He had the "gift," playing the banjo and singing hymns, many he wrote himself. In 1910, Jenkins came to Atlanta to preach, supporting himself by selling newspapers at Five Points. He became a well-known downtown character. In 1919, he married Frances Eskew, a local singer, widowed with two daughters. The Jenkins Family sang at churches and revivals. On August 14, 1922, the group debuted on WSB Radio. Andy sang sacred songs and played the trombone. The family quickly became a mainstay on the station's midday music programs.

The Jenkins Family caught the ear of Polk Brockman. The twenty-four-year-old Brockman had established the city's first phonograph section in his grandfather's furniture store on Decatur Street. He added "radio sets" and was among the first to grasp the crossover possibilities. Brockman was a talent scout for New York–based Okeh (Okay) Records, known for its "race records" featuring black jazz and blues performers. The label also recorded traditional gospel music, adding the Jenkins Family. Today, Brockman

The Jenkins family. From Special Collections and Archives, Georgia State University Library. *Courtesy of Mary Lee Eskew Bowen.*

remains a controversial figure, posthumously accused of conning rustic songwriters into selling the rights to their lyrics and music for practically nothing. Brockman has been compared to a "strip-miner."[70] Blind Andy's stepdaughter, Irene Spain Futrelle, is quite blunt: "When I get to thinking how Mr. Brockman gypped those poor ignorant Negroes and all the rest of us who made records or worked in any capacity for him...oh it makes me almost indignant."[71] Andy Jenkins received as little as five dollars for lyrics that Brockman parlayed into national hits for stars like Jimmie Rodgers.

Andy Jenkins wrote all manner of songs, both sacred and secular, but was known for his "tragedy songs," also called "news ballads." The most famous was "The Ballad of Floyd Collins." A legendary spelunker, Collins had gotten trapped in Kentucky's Sand Cave in 1924. For two weeks, the nation followed the rescue effort until word came that Collins was dead. Brockman went to Jenkins and urged him to write a song capturing this heartbreaking event. Andy's words were recorded by Atlanta's Fiddlin' John Carson for Okeh Records. Brockman, who "owned" the song, sold it to Columbia Records, where a more polished version was recorded by "city-billy" Vernon Dalhart. It became the best-selling Columbia record up to that time.[72]

Brockman was eager for a follow-up. Of course, song-worthy tragedies don't happen every week. But Andy had more unrecorded material ready at hand. "Daddy made songs similarly to the mill grinding out wheat," recalled his stepdaughter. In April 1925, Okeh released a two-sided record. On one side was "Little Mary Phagan," of course, the name of the victim in the Leo Frank case. On the reverse side was "The Fate of Frank DuPre." The lyrics were written around the time of the trial, inspired by the headline "MEET ME IN HEAVEN." Andy recalled sitting on his porch steps, coming up with the words. Inside, he banged out the melody on the piano while Irene transcribed it all.

I want all my buddies and I want my friends,
To take this warning from me:
Stop your drinking and live like men,
Don't live like Frank DuPree.

Come here, buddies, oh, come here quick,
I'll tell you what DuPree has done;
Followed the movie and a sporting life,
Until his race is run.

He went to Atlanta with his sweetheart fair,
He walked into a jewelry store;
Took him a diamond while standing there,
But he'll never take no more.

Took that diamond and he left that shop,
He walked out on that street;
Pulled his pistol and he shot that cop,
He laid him dead at his feet.

He jumped in a flivver and he left that town,
To make his getaway;
But he longed for his sweetheart, but she didn't come round,
So he could not stay away.

They had him arrested and he went to trial;
The judge at last did say.
"Though Frank DuPree is nothing but a child,
He's thrown his life away."

Come here, Poppa, come here quick,
And see the last of your son;
See what the smoking of a vile cigarette
And the sporting life has done.

Come here, Betty, listen to me,
Take these parting words I say,
Take this message for Frank DuPree,
And meet him in Heaven someday.[73]

Jenkins recorded the song in 1925 for Okeh (Okeh Records 40446, 1925), but Dalhart (and Brockman) had greater national success on Columbia (Columbia 15042-D, 1925), selling ninety thousand records.

Meanwhile, a separate group of songwriters had discovered the story of Frank and Betty. In 1926, at the University of North Carolina, Dr. Howard Odum and Guy Johnson published *Negro Workaday Songs*, a collection of songs "current in certain areas in North Carolina, South Carolina, Tennessee and Georgia during the years 1924–25."[74] Among these "bad man ballads" was "Betty Tol' DuPree." (The "DuPree" spelling has been adopted for history.)

DuPree was a bandit,
He was so brave and bol',
He stoled a diamond ring
For some of Betty's jelly roll.

Betty tol' DuPree,
"I want a diamond ring."
DuPree tol' Betty,
"I'll give you anything."

DuPree tol' the judge,
"I am not so brave and bol',
But all I wanted
Was Betty's jelly roll."

The judge tol' DuPree,
"Jelly roll's gonna be your ruin."
"No, no, judge, for that is
What I've done quit doin'."

The judge tol' DuPree,
"I believe you quit too late,
Because it is
Already your fate."

Odum and Johnson knew of the Jenkins recording, noting the obvious: "There is little similarity of expression between the white version and the Negro one." Whereas Jenkins made it plain—"Don't live like Frank DuPre"—the songwriters in the "bad man" tradition stood with the culprit. The onus shifts to the system (the judge, bail, jail and the noose) but also to Betty. The judge lectures DuPre: "Jelly roll's gonna be your ruin." "Jelly roll" was well-established American black slang for the female genitalia. "This term as used by the lower-class Negro stands for the vagina, or for the female genitalia in general, and sometimes for sexual intercourse. Its use among Negroes of the lower class is so extensive that few will deny its meaning."[75] The chain gang and roadhouse singers saw Frank as another victim of the irresistible draw of the "jelly roll." Whereas Blind Andy's version has all but disappeared, the musical legend of "Betty Tol' DuPree" endures today.[76]

What about these two white teenagers caught the interest of these musicians? Actually, the blues singer Brownie McGhee, who recorded the song in the 1950s, thought it was the story of "a Negro youth in love with a white girl and who tried to rob her a diamond ring."[77] But McGhee aside, blues historian Paul Oliver writes, "The appeal of a good tune and a strong theme [transcended] race barriers."[78] Frank's story was a familiar one. What man hadn't felt the pressure to find money to pay the rent, put food on the table or, yes, even pilfer the biggest diamond ring in the window? It took a brave and bold man to do what DuPre did. He killed a cop and made the others look like boneheads. But once captured, he was crushed by "the law."

And he hanged. By the 1930s, it was plain that the race of the dramatis personae had ceased to matter. It was just Betty and DuPree.

The first blues recordings of the song were made in 1930. Kingfish Bill Tomlin's version does not survive but is memorable for the unique reference to DuPre's murder of a "one-eye," a slur amongst the criminal classes for the Pinkerton agency, whose logo was the eye that never sleeps.[79] But the song that truly launched the "DuPree Blues" was recorded by "Blind Willie" Walker (1896–1933), "the most celebrated guitarist in South Carolina." Walker was from Greenville, sixty miles north of Abbeville. In December 1930, he came to Atlanta's Columbia studio on Peachtree with accompanist Sam Brooks. The story was told in the classic AAB style, with the first line of each stanza repeated, while Brooks added plaintive falsetto responses ("Oh, Baby," "Oh, Sugar," etc.) as the feeling moved him:

Betty told DuPree, "I wants me a diamond ring."
"Now listen, Mama. Your daddy bring you most anything."

He had to kill a policeman, and he wounded a 'tective too.
"See here, mama, what you caused me to do."

Hired him a taxi, said "Can't you drive me back to Maine?
I've done a hanging crime, and I don't never feel ashamed."

Standing there wondering, will a matchbox hold my clothes?
Said, "A trunk was too big [indecipherable] the load."

Arrested poor DuPre, and placed him in the jail.
Yea, the mean old judge refused to sign him any bail.

Wrote a letter to Betty, and this is the way the letter read:
"Come home to your daddy, I'm almost dead."

Betty went to the jailer, crying, "Mr. Jailer, please.
Please Mr. Jailer, let me see my used-to-be."[80]

Maine? The dictionary contains few words rhyming with Chattanooga, but Tennessee afforded possibilities. Still, blues singers rarely held any compelling interest in strict historical accuracy. In later recordings, Frank's gun was frequently called a .44 in order to rhyme with "jewelry store."

Oliver reminds us that "black singers seem to have a genius for extending, elaborating and reconstructing" their lyrics to suit the stories they wished to tell.[81]

After Walker, the song was recorded regularly. The African American jazz vocalist Georgia White, from Sandersville, the hometown of Governor Hardwick, recorded the song twice for Decca Records, tidying up the geography somewhat:

> *He got in a taxi and went down to Memphis, Tennessee.*
> *When he got there, detectives was waiting for DuPree.*[82]

While not strictly accurate, at least it was in the correct state. In 1936, White, with a band featuring future legend Les Paul, then using the name "Red Rhubarb," added more detail:

> *He went to Detroit, and there to get his mail.*
> *When he got there, the law was on his trail.*[83]

White artists also covered the song in the 1930s. In 1937, Woody Herman did the vocals while the Thundering Herd played a "blues fox trot" arrangement. Another big-band singer, Teddy Grace, described as "a white woman who sounded black,"[84] recorded it in 1939. Her version refers to DuPree being locked up in the "Big Rock Jail," the local black slang for the Tower.

By this time, no one had any claim to the song. "Betty Tol' DuPree" had quickly achieved "traditional" status, with varying lyrics and "facts." The father-and-son research team of John and Alan Lomax visited jails, sharecropper shacks, roadhouses and other locations collecting traditional songs for their book, *Our Singing Country: Folk Songs and Ballads*.[85] Their version of the song ran to twenty-three verses and included a fanciful shootout in Memphis and more dead policemen in Chicago. In 1936, the Lomaxes recorded "The DuPree Blues" as sung by Walter Roberts, a black inmate at the Raiford, Florida state prison farm. On a note card in the Library of Congress, Lomax wrote, "The words from Langston Hughes who heard it that year in Cleveland."[86] (More from the Harlem poet later.)

The discography of the DuPree blues is lengthy and impressive, including versions from Sonny Terry and Brownie McGee in 1952 and Josh White in 1956. A version was even recorded in Britain, where skiffle singer Lonnie Donegan released "Betty, Betty, Betty."

"Betty and Dupree" by Chuck Willis, Atlantic Records. *Author's collection.*

The biggest commercial success came in 1957. Chuck Willis was a black house painter discovered by a white DJ at Atlanta's WGST. Willis, known as the "King of the Stroll" (complete with a jeweled turban), became a racial crossover star for Atlantic Records. The DuPre song followed up his number-one hit "C.C. Rider." Willis, backed by King Curtis on sax, recorded "Betty and DuPree" on October 30, 1957. But Willis's "slow and sensual" version is a completely nonviolent one. Betty wants a ring, and DuPre agrees to *buy (!)* one for her if she will agree to be his wife. All ends happily:

Betty told DuPree, "Yes, I will be your wife."
He said, "You will, pretty baby, and I'm yours the rest of my life."[87]

That was it—no mention of a shooting or a dead policeman. In 2006, Smithsonian Folkways released a collection entitled *Classic African American Ballads*, including Josh White's recording of "Betty and DuPree." Producer Barry Lee Pearson, in the liner notes, contrasted White's version with Willis's, describing the latter's version as a "schmaltzy love song." Pearson suggested that the nonviolent tone of Willis's record was "possibly" influenced by the negative reaction to Lloyd Price's contemporaneous "Stagger Lee."[88] A similar "outlaw ballad," the song was based on a St. Louis murder. After an argument over a dice game, Stagger Lee went home, got his .44 and returned to shoot a man dead despite the victim's plea that he had "a very, very sickly wife." It was said that influential music promoters, including Dick Clark, were uncomfortable about how white audiences would respond to songs about blacks with guns. Therefore, the legend is that Price agreed to change the lyrics to get on Clark's *American Bandstand*.[89] In the bowdlerized version, Stagger Lee and Billy argue over a girl, and without gunplay, she returns to Stagger Lee with all ending well.

Whatever problems Lloyd Price may have had with "Stagger Lee," they had no influence on Chuck Willis's recording. Chuck Willis died in Atlanta on April 10, 1958, eight months before the *Bandstand* controversy. Pearson believes that Willis's sanitized dance-oriented version was the result of Atlantic Records "kowtowing to concern over teenage morals." In March 1958, Willis's schmaltzy number peaked at number fifteen on the R&B chart. A month later, at the age of thirty-three, he died from a ruptured ulcer blamed on bad barbecue.[90]

By the early 1960s, the stroll was passé. Folk music was ascendant in those pre-Beatles years. The unexpurgated DuPre story was revived amidst the renewed popularity for "bad men ballads" and songs of the downtrodden. New recordings came from Dave Van Ronk; the Limeliters; Peter, Paul and Mary; Harry Belafonte; and the Brothers Four.

In the late '60s, the now-legendary tale received surely its best-known modern iteration when performed and recorded by the Grateful Dead. The first performance of "DuPree's Diamond Blues" was at the Fillmore East in New York in February 1969. The song appeared on the album *Aoxomoxoa* that June. According to *The Complete Annotated Grateful Dead Lyrics*,[91] Jerry Garcia and Robert Hunter reworked the old traditional lyrics (although Hunter admits he was drunk during the process).[92] Garcia considered the song one of his favorites, in the great tradition of all those "'don't take your gun to town'–type tunes."[93]

Well, you know son, you just can't figure,
First thing you know, you're gonna pull that trigger.

And it's no wonder your reason goes bad,
Jelly roll will drive you stone mad.
Same old story, and I know it's been told,
Some like jelly jelly, some like gold.
Many a man's done a terrible thing
Just to get baby a shiny diamond ring.[94]

Maybe Chuck Willis's stroll classic played some summer night on an Amarillo transistor radio. But Robert Blaustein is pretty certain that Betty/ Margaret never heard any of this music. She wasn't a musical person, he recalled, and she didn't listen to the radio much.[95] But if he is mistaken and Betty was aware of the tradition, she surely understood that time had not been kind to her. We recall one of DuPre's lawyers who bemoaned the fact that his naïve client ever met such a "forbidden woman." With words that were "smoother than oil," she pleaded, "Baby, I want a diamond ring." Clearly, that is the message in the traditional blues canon. Betty is an Eve-like figure, "bitter as wormwood, sharp as a two-edged sword." As Blind Willie Walker sang as far back as 1930, "See here, mama, what you done caused me to do." The facts, of course, do not exactly jibe with the legend. Betty did not make Frank fall. Frank was already a "bad man." He had robbed a kinsman, and he had already pinched two rings from a jeweler. He owned that pocket pistol before he ever met Betty. But no matter to the lyricist or poet.

On April 12, 1941, the *Afro-American*, a Baltimore newspaper, carried a poem entitled "Ballad of the Killer Boy" by Langston Hughes. The details of the poem are familiar. The unnamed narrator relates how he agreed to get "a diamond or two" for his girlfriend. Hughes identifies her as "Bernice," but the debt to the story of Betty and DuPre is obvious. A getaway Packard is even mentioned. As already seen, Hughes was aware of the Atlanta crime as early as 1936. The narrator's closing words are stark and damning:

Now they've locked me
In the death house.
I'm gonna die!
Ask that woman,
She knows why.[96]

It was indeed a fateful day when Frank heard the siren sound of Betty Andrews playing her piano at the Childs Hotel. "Jelly roll will drive you stone mad."

Notes

1. Franklin Garrett, *Atlanta and Environs, Volume 2: A Chronicle of Its People and Events, 1880s–1930s* (Athens: University of Georgia Press, 1969), 409.
2. Calculating the comparative purchasing value of the dollar is an inexact science. The author consulted http://www.davemanuel.com/inflation-calculator.php.
3. *Times Independent* (Moab, UT), "Swindlers Net Near Million," June 30, 1921.
4. Charles Frederick Carter, "The Lynching Infamy," *Current History* 15, no. 6 (March 1922), 897.
5. Robert Murphy, "The Depression You've Never Heard Of: 1920–1921," *The Freeman*, December 2009, 24.
6. Buddy Sullivan, *Georgia: A State History* (Charleston, SC: Arcadia Publishing, 2010), 154.
7. Meredith Wilson, *The Music Man*, 1957.
8. Frederick Lewis Allen, *Only Yesterday* (Baltimore, MD: John Wiley & Sons, 1997), 189.
9. *Atlanta Constitution*, "Moonshiners Keep Busy on Job Despite Activity of Dry Agents," August 22, 1921, 5.
10. Ernest Rogers, *Peachtree Parade* (Atlanta, GA: Tupper and Love Inc., 1956), 13.
11. "Governor—Convict and Fugitive Records—Applications for Clemency, 1858–1942 RCB9807: 1858–1942 - Dubberly, H.R. through DuPre, Whit," (DuPre, Frank, Folder 2), Georgia Archives, University System of Georgia, Morrow, GA.
12. Frank DuPre, "Request for Navy Discharge," February 17, 1921. Courtesy of Mark Lomax, a DuPre descendant.
13. Garrett, *Atlanta and Environs*, 257.
14. "Pool Rooms and Similar 'Hangouts' for Men," *Studies in American Social Conditions, Vols. 8–9* (Madison: University of Wisconsin, 1915) 79–80.
15. *Abercrombie & Fitch Catalogue and Price List* (New York, 1907), 174.
16. The different routes from Atlanta to Chattanooga (Nos. 268 or 269) can be consulted in *The Automobile Blue Book Vol. 6, 1919*, 303–06.
17. The author acknowledges the assistance of Jim Balfour of the National Packard Museum, Warren, OH.

18. Howard Preston, *Dirt Roads to Dixie: Accessibility and Modernization in the South* (Knoxville: University of Tennessee Press, 1991).

19. *Atlanta Constitution*, June 11, 1916, 5.

20. Chattanooga African American Museum, *Chattanooga: Black America Series* (Charleston SC: Arcadia Publishing, 2005).

21. Sir John Fielding, *A Plan for Preventing Robberies within Twenty Miles of London* (London, 1755), 15.

22. Wendy Woloson, *In Hock: Pawning in America from Independence through the Great Depression* (Chicago: University of Chicago Press, 2009).

23. Adrian Deane, "American Manhunters," *Startling Detective Adventures* 24, no. 139 (February 1940), 26. The author thanks T.O. Sturdivant III, grandson of the detective, for providing a copy.

24. *St. Petersburg Times*, "Writing Is a Trait of Serial Killers," October 22, 2002, 13.

25. Dan Austin quoting Peter Gavrilovich of the *Detroit Free Press*, http://historicdetroit.org/building/federal-building.

26. Anne Westbrook Green, "H.A. Allen: The Lawyer and the Man," *The Journal of Southern Legal History* 16, no. 1 and 2 (2008), 119.

27. Robert Burns, *I Am a Fugitive from a Georgia Chain Gang!* (Athens: University of Georgia Press, 2011), 22–23.

28. *Atlanta Georgian and News*, "Condemned Negro Wills His Body to Physician," May 24, 1911, 1.

29. "Governor—Convict and Fugitive Records," (DuPre, Frank, Folder 7).

30. John W. Ham, "Doubling a Church Membership in Four Years," *Moody Institute Bible Monthly* 22 (February 1922), 812–13.

31. "Planning of the Fulton County Courthouse," *Architecture and Building* 48 (1916), 23–28.

32. The Code of the State of Georgia (1910), Article 1 §67: Voluntary Manslaughter.

33. Ibid., Article 19 §1036: Prisoner's Statement.

34. *Ferguson v. Georgia* (365 U.S. 570).

35. Rogers, *Peachtree Parade*, 47.

36. The Code of the State of Georgia (1910), Article 1 §63: Murder, Punishment.

37. Gregory Freeman, *Lay This Body Down: The 1921 Murders of Eleven Plantation Slaves* (Chicago: Chicago Review Press, 2002).

38. A lengthy (though incomplete) list of executions in Georgia was compiled by Espy and Smykla. See http://www.deathpenaltyinfo.org/documents/ESPYstate.pdf.

39. Robert Martin, *Hero of the Heartland: Billy Sunday and the Transformation of American Society* (Bloomington: Indiana University Press, 2002).

40. E-mail from Robert Martin, December 18, 2012.

41. "Governor—Convict and Fugitive Records," (DuPre, Frank, Folder 3).

42. *Atlanta Constitution*, "Ridley Will Aid in Fight for Life of DuPre: Great Congregation Hears His Plea for Mercy for Bandit," April 22, 1922, 1.

43. *Wichita Daily Times* (Wichita Falls, TX), "Heartless Vampire or an Abused Angel?" April 23, 1922, 21.

44. *DuPre v. The State* (Georgia Reports 153, 798–826).

45. "Governor—Convict and Fugitive Records," (DuPre, Frank, Folders 1–8).

46. *Atlanta Constitution*, "Mrs. Vinson Sentenced to Hang July 28 Although Prosecution Only Asked Life Term," June 4, 1922, 1.

47. Dudley Siddal, "Why Woman Must Give Life on Gallows in Spite of Plea Made by State Prosecutor," *Charleston Daily Mail*, July 2, 1922, 3.

48. Ralph Jones, "Silhouettes: Memories of a Crime," *Atlanta Constitution*, April 7, 1943, 16.

49. James Cook, *The Governors of Georgia, 1754–2004* (Macon, GA: Mercer University Press, 2005), 220–22.

50. R. Volney Riser, *Defying Disfranchisement: Black Voting Rights Activism in the Jim Crow South* (Baton Rouge: Louisiana State University Press, 2010), 98.

51. "In the Southern Field," *New Outlook* 138 (September 24, 1924), 109.

52. Nancy McLean, *Behind the Mask of Chivalry: The Making of the Second Ku Klux Klan* (New York: Oxford University Press, 1994), 18. Also see Clement Charlton Moseley, *The Political Influence of the Ku Klux Klan in Georgia, 1915–1925* (Statesboro: Georgia Southern College, 1965).

53. The author acknowledges Lauren Hamblin, director of Alumnae Services at Wesleyan College, Macon, GA (August 31, 2012).

54. "Governor—Convict and Fugitive Records," (DuPre, Frank, Folder 1).

55. James Clarke, "Without Fear or Shame: Lynching, Capital Punishment and the Subculture of Violence in the American South," *British Journal of Political Science* 28, no. 2 (April 1998), 287.

56. Donald E. Wilkes, "Sentenced to Death," http://www.law.uga.edu/dwilkes_more/7sentenced.html.

57. See also the 1886 British government's "Scale of Drops" in Timothy Vance Kaufman-Osborn, *From Noose to Needle: Capital Punishment and the Late Liberal State* (Ann Arbor: University of Michigan Press, 2002), 88.

58. Garrett, *Atlanta and Environs*, 794. The author reluctantly notes Garrett's erroneous statement that Frank DuPre was "the last person hanged in Atlanta."

59. http://www.nationalregister.sc.gov/abbeville/S10817701013/.

60. The debate continues in the present-day case of Georgia death row inmate Warren Hill, guilty of two murders. Hill was stated to have an IQ of 70. In October 2013, the U.S. Supreme Court refused to halt his scheduled execution on the grounds that Hill was "mentally disabled." The execution was subsequently delayed for reasons unrelated to Hill's mental capacity. Hill remains on death row in 2014.

61. Vic Gatrell, *The Hanging Tree: Execution and the English People, 1770–1868* (Oxford, UK: Oxford University Press, 1996).

62. Georgia State Office of Planning and Analysis, "A History of the Death Penalty in Georgia: Executions by Year, 1924–2012," January 2013.

63. *Pinkerton v. Walker*, 157 Ga. 548.

64. Rolfe Edmonson, "Frank DuPre's Ghost Returns to Tower," *Atlanta Journal Magazine*, September 16, 1923.

65. Atlanta City Directory, 1943.

66. Robert Blaustein, conversation with author, December 27, 2013.

67. Ibid.

68. *Amarillo Daily News* (Amarillo, TX), June 28, 1972, 12. Courtesy of Mark Lomax.

69. Zell Miller, *They Heard Georgia Singing* (Macon, GA: Mercer University Press 1996), 160–62; Charles K. Wolfe, "Frank Smith, Andrew Jenkins, and Early Commercial Gospel Music," *American Music* 1, no. 1 (Spring 1983): 49–59.

70. Richard Peterson, *Creating County Music: Fabricating Authenticity* (Chicago: University of Chicago Press, 1997).

71. Irene Spain Futrelle to Archie Green, March 11, 1965. Archie Green Collection (Folders 1102–09), Southern Folklife Collection, Wilson Library, UNC Chapel Hill.

72. Archie Green, *Only a Miner: Studies in Recorded Coal-Mining Songs* (Champaign: University of Illinois Press, 1972), 123–34.

73. Andrew Jenkins, D.K. Wilgus Papers #20003, Southern Folklife Collection, Wilson Library, UNC Chapel Hill.

74. Howard Odum and Guy Johnson, *Negro Workaday Songs* (Chapel Hill: University of North Carolina Press, 1926) 55–59.

75. Johnson as quoted in Alfonso Wilson Hawkins, *The Jazz Trope: A Theory of African American Literary and Vernacular Culture* (Lanham, MD: Scarecrow Press, 2008) 161.

76. Chris Smith, "A Hangin' Crime: A Balladic Blues and the True Story Behind It, Parts 1 and 2," *Blues & Rhythm* 95 (February 1995) 4–7 and 96 (March 1995) 4–8.

77. Quoted in Smith, "A Hangin' Crime," *Blues & Rhythm* 96, 8.

78. Paul Oliver, *Songsters and Saints: Vocal Traditions on Race Records* (Cambridge, UK: Cambridge University Press, 1984), 255.

79. Smith, "A Hangin' Crime," *Blues & Rhythm* 96, 5.

80. Blind Willie Walker, "DuPree Blues," Columbia Records (14578-D).

81. Oliver, *Songsters and Saints*, 256.

82. "DuPree Blues," Decca 7100 (1935).

83. "New DuPree Blues," Decca 7209 (1936).

84. Derek Jenkins, "Teddy Grace: Once Lost, Now Found," *The Oxford American* 58, Ninth Annual Southern Music Issue, 2007.

85. John Avery Lomax and Alan Lomax, *Our Singing Country: Folk Songs and Ballads* (Mineola, NY: Dover Publications, 1941), 329–30.

86. Checklist of recorded songs in the English language in the Archive of American folk song to July, 1940: Alphabetical list with geographical index, Volume 1, 89, Library of Congress.

87. "Betty and DuPree," words and music by Chuck Willis. (Atlantic Records 45-1168, 1958)

88. http://media.smithsonianfolkways.org/liner_notes/smithsonian_folkways/SFW40191.pdf.

89. Art Peters, "Off the Main Stem," *Philadelphia Tribune*, December 23, 1958, 5.

90. *Baltimore Afro-American*, "Singer Chuck Willis Dies after Operation," April 12, 1958, 2.

91. David Dodd and Alan Trist, eds., *The Complete Annotated Grateful Dead Lyrics* (New York: Simon & Schuster 2005), 70–73.

92. Quoted in Oliver Trager, *The American Book of the Dead* (New York: Fireside Books, 1997), 106.

93. Blair Jackson, *Garcia: An American Life* (New York: Penguin 2000), 158.

94. "DuPree's Diamond Blues," Robert Hunter, Jerry Garcia. *Garcia/Hunter Songbook: Songs of the Grateful Dead* (Los Angeles: Alfred Music Publishing Company, 2007).

95. Blaustein, conversation with author, December 27, 2013.

96. *Baltimore Afro-American*, "Ballad of the Killer Boy," April 12, 1941, 7. Italics are Hughes's. See also *The Collected Poems of Langston Hughes* (New York: Random House, 1994), 254.

Sources and Acknowledgements

This book relies heavily on the contemporary detailed accounts in Atlanta's three daily newspapers from December 15, 1921, to September 2, 1922. The *Atlanta Constitution*, the *Atlanta Journal* and the *Atlanta Georgian* can be consulted at the Atlanta Public Library, the Atlanta History Center and the Woodruff Library at Emory University. The University of Georgia Library in Athens holds the cited out-of-town Georgia papers. National papers were consulted at the Library of Congress. Additional research was done at the Wilson Library at UNC Chapel Hill and the South Caroliniana Library in Columbia.

For assistance with images, I wish to thank Steve Engerrand at the Georgia Archives in Atlanta (Morrow), Steve Fleming with Georgia State University's Special Collections and Andy De Loach at the Atlanta History Center.

I want to give special thanks to Mrs. Anne Westbrook Green, Henry Allen's granddaughter, who assisted me with biographical information and provided an excellent photograph of the attorney. T.O. Sturdivant III sent me his grandfather's published account of a career as a "manhunter." Mark Lomax, a California attorney and fourth cousin, once removed, of Frank DuPre, provided important leads to tracing Betty Andrews's marriage with Maurice Blaustein. He also supplied the contact information for Robert Blaustein. Of course, I thank the latter for his time and information.

Bibliographical information for the books consulted can be found in the endnotes. Anyone who seeks to learn more about "old Atlanta" must begin with Franklin Garrett's exhaustive *Environs*.

Two helpful digitized sources were the 1921 Atlanta City Directory (https://archive.org/details/atlantacitydirec1921atla) and the Georgia

Code of 1910 (https://archive.org/details/codeofstateofgeo02prepGeorgia Code 1910).

For genealogy and census data, ancestry.com (a pay site) can be helpful.

For the final chapter, I consulted Wayne Daniel's *Pickin' on Peachtree: A History of Country Music in Atlanta* and Chris Smith's vital "A Hangin' Crime: A Balladic Blues and the True Story Behind It, Parts 1 and 2," *Blues & Rhythm* 95 (February 1995) 4–7 and 96 (March 1995) 4–8.

Finally, I thank my wife, Kathleen McGraw, for her interest, her forbearance, her proofreading and her unrelenting support.

Index

INDEX

E

Eskridge, Dr. Frank 51, 52, 87

F

Felton, Rebecca 107
Fenn, Frank 12, 32, 34, 35
Folsom, Dr. Spencer 12, 100
Foster, Louis 46, 52, 54, 57, 66, 96
Frank, Leo 48, 79, 111
Fridell, Henry 68, 69, 74
Fulton County Jail (the Tower) 48, 51,
    54, 56, 68, 69, 70, 71, 75, 76,
    77, 78, 80, 88, 89, 95, 96, 97,
    99, 100, 105, 107, 108, 115

G

Gasque, Reverend G.W. 91, 96, 98,
    99, 108
Geoghan, Vincent 44, 72, 73
Georgia Prison Commission 79, 81
Georgia Supreme Court 62, 76, 80, 106
Grateful Dead 117
Great Southeastern Fair 21, 51, 104
Guillebeau, Len 44, 72

H

Hackett, Chief Wm 32, 39, 106
Hale, J.T. 55, 58, 74
Ham, Reverend J.W. 53, 54, 57, 58, 63,
    66, 71, 72, 82, 104
Harding, Presisdent Warren G 21, 93
Hardwick, Governor Thomas 38, 45,
    51, 70, 71, 82, 84, 85, 86, 87,
    89, 91, 92, 93, 100, 101, 102,
    103, 104, 107, 115
Harrison, Fred 73
Heyward, Izzard 46, 66
Hinton, Howard 105
Hudson, Glen 91, 102
Hughes, Langston 115, 118
Humphries, Judge John 72, 73, 75, 77,
    78, 108

J

Jenkins, Andy
    Jenkins family 109, 110, 111, 112, 113

K

Kaiser's Jewelry Store 10, 12, 15, 26,
    27, 29, 31, 32, 33, 35, 39, 40,
    42, 47, 57, 58, 59, 63, 64, 72,
    73, 84
Keeler, O.B. 57, 61
Kelly, "Dirt Track" 13
Key, Mayor James 12, 16, 36, 41
Kimball House 10, 11, 12, 47, 48, 59,
    60, 61, 86
Ku Klux Klan 36, 71, 72, 86, 97,
    102, 104

L

Lomax, John and Alan 115
Lowry, Sheriff James 70, 81, 89, 97,
    98, 100
Loyless, Tom 92, 101

M

Mason, Newell 87, 88, 91
Mathews, Judge Henry 55, 56, 57, 59,
    60, 65, 66, 67, 68, 69, 74, 75,
    76, 77
McDonald, Luke 93, 96, 97, 98
McGhee, Brownie 113
Meyers, Arthur 105
Mikell, Bishop H.J. 80

N

Napier, Viola 104
Norfolk, VA 14, 32, 33, 34, 35, 36, 37,
    40, 65

O

Osburn, Mrs. Eula 82, 93, 97, 98, 104

About the Author

Tom Hughes was a radio journalist and morning host in Atlanta for over thirty years and is a member of the Georgia Radio Hall of Fame. He has resided in in-town Atlanta since 1977. This is his second book exploring a true crime from Atlanta's past. The first was *Rich Georgian Strangely Shot: Eugene Grace, "Daisy of the Leopard Spots" and the Great Atlanta Shooting of 1912* (McFarland 2012).